FINDING HEARTSTONE

Caitlin Press Inc.
8100 Alderwood Road,
Halfmoon Bay, BC V0N 1Y1
www.caitlin-press.com

Text and cover design by Vici Johnstone
Front cover sketch of Heartstone Lodge by Gordon Lafleur
Printed in Canada

Caitlin Press Inc. acknowledges financial support from the Government of Canada and the Canada Council for the Arts, and the Province of British Columbia through the British Columbia Arts Council and the Book Publish- er's Tax Credit.

Canada Council    Conseil des Arts      BRITISH COLUMBIA      Funded by the        Canada
for the Arts      du Canada             ARTS COUNCIL          Government
                                                              of Canada

Library and Archives Canada Cataloguing in Publication

Finding Heartstone : a taste of wilderness / Cathy Sosnowsky.
Sosnowsky, Cathy, author.
Canadiana 20200258893 | ISBN 9781773860343 (softcover)
LCSH: Sosnowsky, Cathy. | LCSH: Sosnowsky, Cathy. —Family. | LCSH:
Outdoor life—British Columbia. | LCSH: Nature, Healing power of. |
LCSH: Parental grief. | LCGFT: Autobiographies.
LCC PS8587.O84 Z46 2020 | DDC C818/.603—dc23

# Finding Heartstone

A TASTE OF WILDERNESS

# Cathy Sosnowsky

CAITLIN PRESS 2020

# CONTENTS

*To Woldy, builder, father, cook, and lover.*

Alex (8), Michael (6) and Tanya (4), on their fourth trip to Hemming Bay.

# PREFACE

If the builders of Heartstone Lodge, Woldy and Vic Sosnowsky, were writing this history, its subtitle would be "A Taste *for* Wilderness," not a taste *of*. My husband and his brother, Vic, are men of action—slow action, it could be said, since the construction of Heartstone Lodge has so far taken over twenty years. Unlike me, they rarely sit still to write. So, I sit and write this story about their dream of constructing a home in the wilderness, in return for their having provided me with every writer's dream: a desk below a window looking out onto a silent forest.

The story of Heartstone Lodge belongs within the larger story of the Hemming Bay Community, a co-operative formed in 1979 to preserve a wilderness sanctuary on East Thurlow Island, located in the northern portion of British Columbia's popular yet treacherous inland waters. The BC coast has known many co-operatives and utopian communities. Most of them did not last for more than a decade. Internal disputes and betrayals tore them apart. But, somehow, the idealistic and sensible Hemming Bay Community founders have managed to keep their dream together for almost forty years.

In the following pages, you will meet some of the characters who lived and worked in Hemming Bay, and some of the animals that live there, but mainly, you will read what I think of as a "redemptive narrative." I borrow the term from Jim Shepard, author of *The Book of Aron*. Shepard writes that all personal narratives are both "self-condemning and self-exonerating." As the narrator of this tale, I blame myself for being a wimp for not having fully embraced the wilderness and its challenges; at the same time, I admire my hanging on until that writing desk was finally placed under Heartstone's upstairs window.

Any recounting of a personal journey must be subjective. My grief over the loss of my three children plays a central role, as does the struggle of keeping together a marriage under stress. A beloved granddaughter joins us at Hemming Bay, and a lost son returns in the final chapter, giving hope for a continuing story.

Although I have checked with most of the people found on these pages regarding their roles, I may have made mistakes in some of the details. If so, I apologize.

The recipes included in these chapters emerge from the narrative. They help define my wish to nourish and to become better connected to my family and community.

Michael and Tanya (with Alex, middle) on their first visit to Hemming Bay.

Sue Chickman and Bob Proice, among the founding members.

# FINDING LIMPETS

When my husband told me we could buy into a wilderness co-op and have a piece of beachfront on an island to ourselves, I said, "Oh, let's do it!" I said it without even seeing East Thurlow Island, somewhere up the BC coast. Woldy had visited it with his brother, Vic, our soon-to-be partner, and they had come back with photos showing a tree-filled, highway-free island with five large lakes and not a building in sight. Overgrown logging roads hinted at a busier history, but at that time, in 1979, it seemed to be a pristine, inviting wilderness.

A group of Seattle environmentalists took the initiative to buy the 232 acres of private land. They came from a range of backgrounds. For example, three of the planners worked for Boeing, the large company that dominated Seattle industry. Two in the group were marine biologists, one was a goat farmer, another an anthropologist, and still another an apple grower. What this mixed bag of twenty shareholders had in common was that they had all read Thoreau and believed in the redemptive power of nature. The youngest of the investors, bearded and in overalls, had visited East Thurlow Island as a Sea Scout. Now in a different uniform (the hippie attire of the 1970s), he wanted to fulfill his boyhood dream of retreating to the forest. His girlfriend, Sue, was already a commune dweller, a lover of goats and granola. Woldy and Vic contributed strong Ukrainian bodies that actually loved labouring. Also, they were the Canadian partners needed to make this purchase legal.

Another thing the founding members shared in the 1970s was a fear of the nuclear arms race. The Seattle area, with its Boeing factory and adjacent military bases, would be a likely target for Soviet planes carrying atomic or hydrogen bombs. Maps for the fallout area from such an attack clearly showed that East Thurlow Island was far enough north to escape any fallout radiation. So, the call of the wild and the fear of nuclear holocaust were prime motivations for the founding of the Hemming Bay Community.

My motivation was much simpler. I loved to swim. I loved watching wildlife programs on TV and wanted to see for myself the living animals in their natural habitats. As a preteen, my favourite book had been *The Call of the Wild*. I imagined that a West Coast island would have wolves, deer, cougars, bears and sea otters. One could dig for clams, go fishing for salmon and cod, or throw down a crab trap. I was familiar with the bounty of the sea from the summers Woldy and I had spent aboard our twenty-six-foot sailboat, a boat that had yet to venture as far north as East Thurlow Island.

After my husband and his brother bought their share of the property, Woldy and I sailed up from Vancouver. Well, mostly we motored, as even at six knots per hour (our max), it took us two days to reach our destination, two hundred miles from our moorage at West Vancouver's Eagle Harbour Yacht Club. Alex, our only child at the time, was three years old. He couldn't swim yet, but I was sure I could teach him at "our" beach. What I didn't know yet was that the northern waters above the Seymour Narrows rapids in the Gulf of Georgia are always ice-cold, even in the summer months. I soon found this out on my first dive off our boat after anchoring in Hemming Bay.

"Eek! Help me out of here!" I screeched, splashing my way

back to the boat's rope ladder.

Woldy was laughing, but Alex looked with alarm at his screaming mother. To assure the boy, I attempted to laugh too.

"Ouch! My forehead hurts!" I complained, as I climbed on board and quickly wrapped myself in a beach towel. No, this was not swimmable water! My first disappointment in my dream of a wilderness paradise.

Back in a warm hoodie and jeans, I asked Woldy to row Alex and me ashore. Two days confined to a twenty-six-foot boat is tough for a three-year-old—and for his mother. We would roam the shore together, collect shells and pretty stones, I thought.

But no! The shores of Hemming Bay consisted only of jagged rocks! No stretches of sand for our youngster to run on, or to build castles. In fact, I mostly had to carry Alex, which intensified the challenge the rugged terrain posed to my own shaky legs. Just when I was about to cry, "This is not what I imagined, not what I dreamed of!" a kingfisher shrieked and dove down about twelve feet in front of us.

"Look, Alex, look! A blue bird!" I cried.

And Alex, who at the age of four would declare that he wanted to be an ornithologist, clapped his hands in excitement.

After more exploring, we hollered for Woldy to come and row us back to the boat, along with a bucket of definitely-not-pretty stones, which were to occupy young Alex for at least half an hour.

"*Boom!*" he shouted, as each rock he threw overboard made a satisfying splash, sending off rings and bubbles.

I clapped and shouted, "Bravo!"

"Mommy go *Boom*!" Alex demanded, his rock pail now empty.

"Not here, hon, not here," I said.

Mommy would go *Boom* further south, in the waters of Desolation Sound, anchored among many visiting sailboats, but not here, dammit, not here.

We had the bay to ourselves for one day and night. Unbelievable, compared to the crowded anchorages where we had stayed on our journey north. As we sipped our nightly brandy in the boat's cockpit, Alex now asleep in the front berth, I forgot about the icy swim and the rocky beach. Multitudes of stars, never seen near city lights, winked down upon us. The boat rocked gently as moonlight played on the water.

The next morning, our new partners in this wilderness co-operative started arriving: by water taxi from Campbell River, by seaplane from Seattle (one of our members actually owned and piloted one), and even by kayak from Rock Bay, the closest launching point for crossing Johnstone Strait. While Alex and Woldy were excited by this commotion (especially the landing of the seaplane not far from our anchorage), I was regretting the loss of the quiet of stargazing and kingfisher watching. With the arrival of representatives of the twenty shareholders, we were no longer Mr. and Mrs. Robinson Crusoe and son, sole possessors of the bay.

Despite my occupation as a teacher of college English, I am basically a shy person. When Alex was about eight, he said to me, "You're not like other mothers. You don't talk on the phone or go have coffee with friends." I guess he got this image of a "typical mom" from TV. It was true. I prepared lessons and marked papers, I played and read with my son, but I didn't keep up with a social circle of friends. Woldy, the garrulous one, got very excited about the arrival of our Hemming Bay partners and their friends. Alex and I stayed on our boat while he rowed ashore to the grassy outcropping where the newcomers were unloading their tents.

Hours passed. I could make out all the busyness on shore and knew that Woldy, who had led many camping trips in his role as principal of an alternative school, would be helping to set up tents and to start cooking fires. Perhaps he had gone into the woods for firewood and it was him swinging the axe that was echoing across the once-silent bay.

My parents had never taken my sister and me camping. They had worked so hard to provide for us that the idea of buying tenting equipment and leaving the city when Vancouver's beaches were our free playgrounds never occurred to them. I did go to Girl Guides for a year, but I never opted to go to camp. I didn't like the idea of sleeping outside with strangers.

Well, ashore were strangers I was going to have to get to know. I couldn't hide out with my child on our boat refuge for the three days allotted for exploring our new, mutually held wilderness.

Woldy had left us at around two in the afternoon and didn't return until six. "Come on!" he said. "We're going to have our first community dinner!"

I would have preferred to cook for the three of us in our little ship's galley, using our two pots and three bright plastic plates and looking out the galley window at the changing colours of the sea. I was also feeling irritable from my four-hour wait, but I didn't want to argue in front of Alex.

"What should I bring?"

"Don't worry. They have lots of food. We'll contribute to tomorrow night's dinner. Come on! Get on!"

"Get on" meant climbing down the rope ladder to our rubber dinghy, first handing Alex down to Woldy's arms. He stood in the dinghy, with his arms outstretched as he precariously balanced his large body to receive our boy. *Gasp!* I didn't know much about seamanship, but I knew you weren't supposed to stand in a little tippy rubber rowboat while holding on to a three-year-old.

We thankfully made it safely to shore and were greeted by the tent colony with gusty hellos. Alex, like his father, was very social, and he was soon running from tent to tent, making himself known and loved. He also attempted to join some older children who were rolling down a grassy bank, yelling, "Downdee, down, down!" I held back, trying to memorize names—I was good at that in the classroom, where students sat in rows and occupied the same seats every time. Oddly, there were three couples named Bob and Sue—how was I ever going to tell them apart? At least I was wearing jeans, like the rest of them, but I felt that my short haircut and horn-rimmed glasses gave me away. I was not a hippie or an outdoorswoman, and although I had a social conscience and had even marched in nuclear protests, I was basically conservative and shy.

The shared food was vegetable stew with cornmeal bread. No store-bought hot dogs here. I was already worrying about what I could bring for tomorrow night's feast. I couldn't go to the store for tofu.

Alone, back on our boat, with Alex tucked in bed in the forward berth, Woldy asked me why I was so silent.

"I don't like it here," I answered.

"What? What don't you like?"

"Shh, don't shout at me; you'll wake Alex, and voices carry over water."

"Okay," he said, now in a lowered tone, "What don't you like?"

"Everything: the cold water, the ugly beach, the too many people, you going off for hours."

"It wasn't hours. And I thought you liked being alone on the boat."

❧

This was the first of many arguments we would have about Hemming Bay. The boat was gently rocking, the multitude of stars were shining, but our different temperaments were pushing us apart: Woldy, the extrovert who loved challenges; me, the introvert who loved comfort and her own space.

Sensing that we needed time apart the next morning, Woldy again left me to join the campers, this time to explore with them the paths and creeks outlined on the map. First, he rowed Alex and me ashore, confident that any bear or cougar nearby would have been frightened off by last night's loud chattering. Again, I brought along a bucket for rock collecting, and fortunately, I had Woldy's Swiss army knife in my pocket. I was well equipped for what Alex and I found in our explorations—multitudes of limpets, also called "Chinese hats," clinging to the undersides of large shore rocks. Remembering that these were listed as edibles in our *How to Cook Your Catch* book, I slipped the knife's edge below a shell's rim before the creature applied suction. *Whoop!* Off it fell—into our bucket.

"More!" Alex chimed. "More!"

And so, we scrambled from rock to rock, filling our bucket half full of squirming, indignant little snails. Back on board, I made our contribution to that night's dinner:

Limpet Escargot

Let the limpets sit in sea water for an hour or so to cleanse themselves of sand.

Boil them in a little water until they are loose from their shells.

Throw the shells back into the sea.

Fry the little morsels in butter and finely chopped garlic.

Serve on crackers.

As Alex and I passed our appetizer around that night to exclamations of, "Where did you find these? They taste like escargot!" I felt I'd taken my first step toward belonging to an island community.

Me and Alex.

# Visiting Serenity Isle

We returned to Hemming Bay the following summer. Alex was four and sturdier on his feet, so when I washed our clothes in the creek that poured into the bay, he was able to splash around, holding on to the rocks when he lost his balance. I enjoyed rowing ashore with our dirty clothes in a black plastic bag with a small bag of laundry detergent (biodegradable, of course) inside it. As I pounded our underwear and T-shirts against the rocks, like I'd seen African women doing on *National Geographic* programs, the romantic in me imagined escaping the modern mechanized world, with all its appliances, gadgets and nuclear weapons.

Years later, as a mother of three (we adopted two children when Alex was eight) and still a college instructor, I suffered from anxiety and exhaustion. When I went to my doctor for help, he asked me to close my eyes and imagine a place where I felt at peace. This clothes-washing scene at the creek came back in vivid detail—the cold, moving water; the slippery rocks underfoot; and especially the little boy splashing beside me, the sun reflecting off his blond head forming a shiny helmet.

On our second visit to the island, there were fewer campers; we had, by now, selected a likely piece of shoreline for our projected home-in-the-woods. Of the 232 acres purchased by the Hemming Bay Community, each of the twenty shareholders could choose a lot along the ocean or lakeshore on which to build. The building had to be situated at least fifty feet from the tide line, leaving trees between it and the water so that the wilderness was preeminent. Any cutting of the lush forest must comply with community guidelines.

Woldy had chosen our "personal use space" with the help of his partner, Vic. They had picked out a lot on the ocean, but I had heard that the large Hemming Lake, on which the community also owned shoreline, was swimmable. I still hadn't seen it.

"Let's look at the lake before we decide," I pleaded. "Maybe we'd rather build there."

As someone who wasn't going to be active in the building project, I really didn't have a right to choose, but Woldy conceded: "Okay, let's look at the lake. We can talk to Vic about it later."

To get to the lake from the bay required a twenty-minute trek uphill on an old logging road, which led to a lagoon. The lagoon, plugged with fallen logs from the days when first-growth forest had been felled, almost a hundred years ago, was not navigable. Luckily, we hadn't trekked there with a canoe on our shoulders. Instead, we bushwhacked our way on a path along the lagoon, me wondering if this was a trail once used by First Nations people.

Alex spent most of the journey on his dad's back in a carrier, with the inevitable question, "Are we there yet?" punctuating the sounds of our boots crunching the undergrowth—this was not a well-used path!

Since we weren't sure where "there" was, it was hard to answer, other than, "Soon, soon."

"When we get home," I said to Woldy on one of our pauses, "I'm going to look up the history of this place."

"Don't worry about history; just keep moving now!"

It took us another twenty minutes to get from the start of the trail at the beginning of the lagoon to the end of the trail, where it opened onto the lake. It was a crystalline scene: a lake that extended for miles, dotted with islands and backed by gentle, tree-covered mountains.

"Wow! Let's build here!" I exclaimed, before even trying the water.

The setting looked so peaceful; here was a place that would nourish the soul. Now, however, we had to cross the lagoon in order to reach the small, sandy beach we could see nestled below a moss-covered rock outcropping. We backtracked to a spot where we had noted a large log crossing the lagoon—apparently meant to be a bridge. Woldy carried Alex across and then coached me: "Don't look down. Just put one foot in front of the other and look at me."

I have a fear of heights. Not that this log was high, but crossing over on it required a kind of confidence that I lacked. Step by step, though, I made it!

Now we scrabbled over a rocky trail that led by natural gradations to the longed-for beach. We quickly discarded our sweaty clothes and waded in. (Alex could now swim, thanks to winter lessons at our community pool.) Yes, indeed, the water was swimmable—cool at first, but as is always said by avid swimmers, "You get used to it!"

Clean and happy, we found sitting ledges on what we now called "our swimming rocks." We seemed absolutely alone on the lake—it was so large that you couldn't see its end, and there was not a building or boat in sight. We nibbled our crackers, and we mixed orange powder with the clean lake water in our Thermos. Spreading our beach towels on the moss, we sunbathed naked, eyes alert for the snakes whose sleep we had disturbed. "Just the garden variety," Woldy assured me when I recoiled from a sliding shape. Fearless and curious, four-year-old Alex tried to catch them.

A purring noise broke our quiet chatter. What? A motorboat on "our" lake? Where was it coming from, and why was it heading directly for us? I pulled my beach towel over my naked torso. Woldy, standing, wrapped his around his waist. Alex, unabashedly nude, started waving at the approaching stranger. As the skiff came closer, I could see that the lone boater was smiling—he didn't look danger-ous or confrontational at all.

"Ahoy, mateys!" he called, when close enough for us to hear, taking his hand off the throttle and saluting.

I saluted back, and Woldy shouted, "Ahoy!"

Alex asked, "What does 'ahoy' mean?"

Our visitor expertly grounded his vessel on the small sandy beach (no longer "our" private beach) and nimbly jumped ashore. A brown shaggy dog, who had been lying unseen on the bottom of the boat, bounded out after him. Alex squealed his delight—he loved all animals.

"Good day for a swim!" the stranger said, and I feared he was about to take off his overalls and join us. No, I could see from the sunburn lines at the neck of his open checkered shirt that this man rarely—if ever—sunbathed. And the laugh wrinkles on his bronzed, leathered face told me that there was no danger here.

"I'm Ron Laidlaw," he said, holding out his hand, reaching down first to shake mine (I hadn't jumped up to greet him), then moving over to shake Woldy's.

Hearing Woldy's name, our new friend said, "Wally?"

"No, Woldy, W-O-L-D-Y—a contraction of Woldemar, the German version of Vladimir, which should be my name."

Oh no, I feared; Woldy was about to launch into his "dis-placed person" story—the tale of his family's escape from Russia as World War II ended and how, after being detained in Germany, where Woldy was born, the family was almost shipped to Peru. That would have kept Ron there as a fresh and captive listener for a long time. I had heard the story many times and was pleased when Ron did not make further enquiries.

Instead, he turned to Alex. "And who's this little sailor?" Ron asked, smiling down at him.

"I'm Alex, and I'm going to be an ornithologist when I grow up." Alex liked to beat new adults to their tiresome questions.

"An ornithologist! Now that's a big word for a little guy!"

"It means birdwatcher," Alex explained. Sometimes adults didn't understand the word "ornithologist" because of Alex's lisp.

"And what brings you three to this far-out lake?"

"We live here," said Alex. "It's our lake."

"Your lake, eh? I thought it was *my* lake."

I would have feared an unpleasant confrontation if it weren't for Ron's smile as he said it.

Woldy stepped in with an explanation: "We're part of the Hemming Bay Community—twenty of us pitched in to buy Lot 440, and we really only live here for a few weeks of the summer. Where do you call home?"

"This here lake is my home. Come, I'll take you to my island. You can see it from here," and he pointed to what looked to me like an unoccupied island. "Serenity Isle, I call it."

*He lives on an island on a lake on an island*, I thought to myself. *Of course it should be called "Serenity Isle!"*

"Sure. Let's go for a ride," said Woldy, without consulting Alex or me. I was still trying to figure out how to crawl into my shorts and tank top without embarrassing myself or our new friend. Alex, meanwhile, had made friends with Buster Brown, laughing as the dog licked his face.

"Why don't you wait in your boat, Ron, while we make ourselves decent?"

"Sure thing, sure thing," said Ron. "Though you look pretty decent to me."

The tin boat had just enough room for the five of us, Alex snuggling in the bow with Buster Brown. Our boy was clearly enjoying the novelty of a fast-moving motorboat, having spent a lot of time asking, "Are we there yet?" on our slow-moving sailboat.

Ron's cedar shake cabin was tucked among trees on the west side of a small island. A few tied-up logs served as a dock. Once ashore and approaching the cabin, we passed a carefully laid-out garden.

*Oh my God*, I thought—*nine bean rows!* If only Yeats could see this. I couldn't wait to find out if Ron knew the poem "The Lake Isle of Innisfree."

I will arise and go now, and go to Innisfree,
And a small cabin build there, of clay and wattles made;
Nine bean-rows will I have there, a hive for the honey-bee,
And live alone in the bee-loud glade.

The poem was rattling round in my head as I counted the bean rows and looked about for a beehive.

Woldy asked Ron question after question about the building of his cabin. Not "clay and wattles," but what Ron called "piss pole" (meaning "straight") cedars for support, salvaged plywood for the walls, corrugated cardboard for insulation, and hand-split cedar shakes for finishing off the exterior walls. What impressed me the most were the shelves of home-canned beans, tomatoes and salmon. Stalks of garlic were hanging from the ceiling to dry. We went out for a closer look at the garden. Woldy asked Ron how he managed to have such lush growth on this unfertile and rocky soil. Ron, pleased to have an admiring audience, explained that the garden was the result of many, many trips to the seashore to gather seaweed, which he mixed with rotted logs and soil dug up from the lakeshore. He sent samples to the Ministry of Agriculture to find out what fertilizer to use.

"Wonderful!" exclaimed Woldy. "These tomatoes would win

prizes at the Chilliwack Fair!" Woldy was brought up in a farming community, and he always grew vegetables wherever we lived.

Grinning broadly, Ron handed me a cloth grocery bag and invited me to help myself to whatever we could use: lettuce, tomatoes, peas, green onions and, of course, beans. On our sea voyages we were always running out of fresh vegetables, especially salad makings, so this was a very much appreciated offer. (Alex loved the line from Rapunzel's pregnant mother: "If I don't get some salad, I will surely die!" We repeated it to him whenever he ignored his fresh greens.) Looking at the grocery bag label, I saw it was from a supermarket in Campbell River. *Ah*, I thought, *Ron must sometimes need things he can't grow; he must sometimes leave his island.*

As I stood on Ron's island, looking over the lake, I wondered about our new venture and future cabin. Although it had always been Woldy and Vic's dream to build a house in the woods, we had not yet taken any steps toward construction and had not decided which of the designated "private use" parcels to claim as ours. So far, two years into the community's founding, only one shareholder had built a private dwelling. Jay Wakefield was a man of some means and had flown in materials and a crew from Seattle by helicopter to build his cabin in just two weeks. On our teachers' salaries, Woldy and I could not afford such a project, but here was Ron, a man of no means, who had built what looked to me like a dream cabin all by himself.

After our tour, Ron offered to ferry us back to our bathing rocks and promised to bring us a potato salad if we were in the same place tomorrow.

"Right! Good! We'll be there," said Woldy. "What can we bring for you?"

"You got any hooch on that fancy sailboat of yours?"

"Sure, sure. What's your poison—whiskey or vodka? And what do you like to mix it with?"

"Mix it? Hell no, I drink my vodka right out of the bottle."

The next day, encouraged, I guess, by the libation we had brought, Ron told us of his life on the bottle, which partly explained why he now sought peace on an isolated island.

"In the city, I was drunk every night. Ended up sleeping on the streets. I preferred bank doorways—I liked the ironic contrast."

I risked asking him if he paid rent on his island.

"No, rent's free. I'm what you call a squatter. I occupy land nobody wants."

Free. He lives for free. He lives freely. Again, I thought about how Yeats would have envied him. Yeats, dreaming of Innisfree while standing "on the pavements grey." Despite enjoying the cultural advantages of city life and a profession I loved, in my "deep heart's core," I envied Ron.

And he made a delicious salad!

## SQUATTER'S POTATO SALAD

Peel, chop up, and boil your potatoes.

When they're cool, mix them with sliced radishes, celery, green onions, chopped hard-boiled eggs (an ingredient Ron purchased—he couldn't raise chickens because of the wolves).

Mix all the veggies with mayo, mustard, salt, pepper, celery seed, chopped parsley.

"Tastes better if you make it the day before," Ron said when he delivered it to us. "And better still with vodka."

Amy pulls up a good one, while Uncle Woldy and cousin Alex laugh in approval.

# CHILDREN SUMMERS

As excited as I was about our lovely swimming spot, the trek to the lake had discouraged me from thoughts of building there. Woldy's determination to build our own cabin—sometime—was reinforced by his visit to Ron's. However, not many of our Hemming Bay Community members could afford or wished to build their own wilderness dwellings. The community therefore decided to build a common-use lodge, levying fees to all members and employing a Vancouver Island builder. There was no problem finding lumber—after all, the group owned over two hundred acres of forest.

A small logging company was hired to fall and mill fir and pine trees not far from the building site. Deciding on a site had proved to be a challenge. There were those who wanted it by the sea, on the grassy knoll where they had first camped. Others preferred access to the lake rather than the ocean, reasoning that access to swimming was more important than a view of the un-swimmable sea. An agreement to build at the mouth of the lake's lagoon was the compromise—a site halfway between the sea and the lake.

An adaptation of a Swiss farmhouse was eventually built, with a sturdy wood stove, a dozen bunk beds, and a large, inviting dining room table with benches for communal dinners. "The Hemming Bay Lodge," as we all came to call it, was a fancy name for a dwelling with rough cedar walls, a bare wooden floor, and bedroom divisions with no doors, just dividing walls reaching about seven feet high. The two "master" bedrooms had planks with foam mattresses to serve as double beds.

A hundred-year-old dam on what was once a creek had been built to raise the lake for the convenience of transporting logs, and it was later modified to enhance salmon migration. We were fortunate to have members with engineering degrees who figured out how to use the dam's water pressure to transport running water to the lodge. A hot shower was possible, once the stove had been burning for a few hours. Except for the necessity of using an outhouse (a septic system was ruled out, as it might contaminate the source of our drinking water), our wilderness experience was becoming quite comfortable.

I still preferred living on our sailboat in the bay. There were too many cooks in the kitchen and often too many in line for the shower or the outhouse. Also, the community had now hired a caregiver to live in the lodge year-round, and whoever it was seemed to have a sense of ownership that we had to tiptoe round. Guide rules were drawn up about booking the lodge for members' use, but there often was an overlap—whoever was there with a booking was not likely to turn away other members as drop-in guests. At times, fourteen people would be dining together, creating chaos in the kitchen. If more than two people had used the shower at night, there would not be hot water until the following evening.

While Woldy, who loves company, would happily pack up our gear from the boat to the lodge and take whatever bed was available, in the years we visited with our only child, Alex, I prevailed with my wish to stay on the boat, joining in for communal meals at the lodge occasionally. Our daily outing from the sailboat was to trek to the swimming rocks at the lake. Now that the lagoon below the lodge had been cleared of the logjam that was left over from early twentieth-century logging, a canoe and a rowboat were kept at its mouth, so our transport to the little beach below the rocks was easy and pleasant. If Vic and his wife, Lee, came to Hemming Bay at the same time as we did, Alex would have a playmate in their daughter, Amy, a half year younger than he. At times Woldy and Alex would take our dinghy and go for fishing excursions to islands near our bay. I was happy to remain on our boat by myself for a few hours, reading a novel while the gentle waves of the bay rocked me. Cod were an easy catch, and what a triumph when they would return with salmon. Clam digging when the tide was low in the cove near our anchorage was a fun occupation for all three of us. Woldy would dig deep holes in the muddy sand, and Alex and I would compete to search out the biggest clams. Some days we would plan a trip to Ron's Serenity Isle, returning with a bagful of his wonderful produce. During the evenings on our anchored sailboat, Alex was content to draw and write in his journal. I brought along a pile of our favourite children's books—*Higglety Pigglety Pop! or There Must Be More to Life*, by Maurice Sendak, was a favourite. It contains the line, "There must be more to life than having everything"—and at that time, I did think I had everything.

But Alex had always wanted a sister or a brother—preferably both. By the time we realized that neither would be forthcoming naturally (though we did try!), I was in my forties—too old to adopt a baby, and anyway, a baby would be too young for Alex. I responded to an article in a series called "Tuesday's Child" in the *Vancouver Sun*, which promoted the adoption of older children. The item pictured an athletic-looking ten-year-old girl who had had "inconsistent parenting" and needed a home. (In retrospect, thinking about her age, I wonder if I was trying to replace the premature baby girl we'd lost two years before Alex's birth.) I wrote to the BC Ministry for Children and Families to tell about our circumstances and inquire about this particular child. A letter came soon after to advise me that it was not recommended to adopt a child who was older than your own birth child. I was also advised to contact the ministry to initiate papers that would lead to a home study. Also, I could go to my local Ministry for Children's office to look at a catalogue of children available for adoption. Much as this idea of shopping for a new child through a catalogue struck me as crass, I went along with it.

I had already convinced Woldy that it was about time we did the paperwork required, when I found a photo of Tanya and Michael in the Ministry for Children's book of "Special Needs Children." Children over two years old were designated as "special needs" because of the assumption that they had already suffered psychologically from the loss of their parents. Other children included had Down syndrome, or they were deaf, incontinent or had other less serious afflictions. Under a photo of each child was an upbeat description of them, followed by a warning. Tanya was described as lively, above her age verbally, and suffering from malnutrition, with a warning that she went too readily to strangers. Michael was described as playful and friendly, but he had a tendency to take things that didn't belong to him. As an orphan, he would have nothing, so I thought of course he would take from others. I was not at all alarmed by the precautions. These children were perfect, as far as I was concerned: A brother and sister at once! And they were just the right ages: Alex was now eight, Michael was about to turn six, and Tanya was four. The children looked pale and thin in the photo, and rather sad, but I fell in love with their images. I brought a reproduced copy of their page home to show Woldy.

"You never said we were going to adopt two," he said. "I agreed to one!"

"Yes, but look, they need each other, and this way they won't feel overwhelmed by the three of us."

"And what are you going to do when they smear shit on the

walls?" asked Woldy. As the principal of a school for high-risk children, he knew that this type of behaviour was entirely possible.

"I'll wipe it off!"

❧

Woldy finally agreed to visit the children at their current foster home, and his heart won over his head. Little Tanya sat on his knee while he read to her from her favourite book, a thin, battered copy of *Snow White and the Seven Dwarfs*. When she chimed in with "hair as black as ebony," we were both impressed. A four-year-old with such a vocabulary! Michael, meanwhile, was playing social worker with Alex in the back yard, pretending to take Alex into his custody.

It turned out that not many families want to adopt two children at once, especially two who are designated as "special needs." Our adoption went through after just one home visit from the social worker and one visit to the children at their foster mom's.

At that time, Tanya and Michael were attending a special daycare for children with emotional problems. Losing their mother to a drug overdose at such young ages designated them as "needy." Since they had been removed from their mother's care (or neglect) a year before we met them, they had lived in three different foster homes. We gladly agreed to continue their attendance at the special daycare and to meet, at first weekly, then biweekly, with the resident child psychiatrist, Carl Rothschild. It was he who thought it would be a good idea for us to continue with our summer plan of boating to Hemming Bay just a few weeks after the children moved in with us. Being confined on a small sailboat for two days, and then in a wilderness lodge together, was bound to be a bonding experience, he said. He said this never having been on a small sailboat himself. He added that he would personally fly up to join us if there was an emergency.

Carl never did have to fly up, but he enjoyed the stories of bonding we shared with him when we got home, such as the time that Michael stumbled into a hornet's nest and had to be cuddled while being doused in calamine lotion—Michael did not like to be touched. Tanya had to sleep with Woldy and me in the front berth of the boat. She was small for her four years, suffering from malnutrition, so she fit in easily. What better way to bond than by sleeping together? The adjustment from a family of three to a family of five was not easy for Alex, though he had been so keen to have siblings. When Michael tried to steal Alex's emblem of the eagle as they were drawing their favourite animals, Alex, aged eight, began to cry.

A clue to how difficult it would be to make these children truly ours was when we tried to get them to sing along with us on the long sailboat journey to Hemming Bay. We sang songs with lyrics like "Would you like to swing on a star?" or "Just what makes that little old ant / Think he'll move that rubber tree plant." Tanya, the verbal one of the pair, did try to sing along. Michael just frowned at us. I asked him why he wouldn't sing. "Those are your songs, not mine!" he said. The song he did sing repeatedly was "Beat It" by Michael Jackson. It was a song we didn't like, and we actually designated limited times for him to chant out "Beat It."

Our first summer holiday with our enlarged family was not easy, whether underway on the boat or staying at the communal lodge once we arrived at Hemming Bay. We discovered that Tanya had a urinary tract problem when she wanted to be carried to the outhouse every half an hour. At first I thought it was because she loved being carried—Carl had explained that because of their lack of nurturing in their early years, our children would often revert to below-age behaviour. Clearly, we had much to learn in our new parenting roles.

The best story we had for Carl was from the last night of our boat journey home. We decided to have a "Gala Night" like they do at the end of cruise ship voyages. Each of us would have to dress up and entertain each other with some kind of performance. We used my lipstick and eyeshadow to paint our faces. Woldy sang silly songs, accompanying himself on the harmonica. Alex did some magic tricks he had been practising. I tried to do the Highland Fling (I had taken lessons as a child), rocking the anchored boat considerably. Woldy had laid out a rope on which Tanya could pretend to be a tightrope walker, and he had coached Michael on a "Mickey the Clown" routine. When it was his turn to perform, it was the first time I had seen Michael looking happy. I wish I could have taken his photo, but that was before digital cameras, and I had run out of film.

In the following summers, we made sure we arranged to share our wilderness time with Vic's family too. Vic and his wife, Lee, also had three children: Amy, just six months younger than Alex, and the twins, Katie and Lena, who were one year younger than Tanya. On these summer vacations (never longer than two weeks), the communal lodge, which we had booked for the Sosnowsky families, resounded with children's shouts and laughter.

A highlight of these holidays was a fishing derby organized by Woldy. The day started with making a sign that indicated the prize categories. There were six children, so there had to be six prizes.

## HEMMING BAY'S ANNUAL FISHING DERBY

Prizes for:
the smallest fish
the prettiest fish
the ugliest fish
the longest fish
the most colourful fish
the funniest fish

Three children, a mix from the two families, went off with Vic in the community's aluminum skiff, and three went with Woldy in a battered old wooden tender. I was left with instructions to open a can of beer and let it sit long enough to go flat. I was also in charge of finding the prizes for when the fisherpeople returned: a chocolate bar (precious at our camp, where there was no corner store); a loonie (which is a one-dollar golden coin, American readers); a package of cards; two shiny fishing lures with feathers; and a fish bonker with a carved eagle for a head, fashioned by Woldy with his handy Swiss knife, and used to put fish out of their misery once they were on board.

Lee and I had a couple of hours of quiet time to read our novels before the fisherpeople returned with their catch. When they did, and the catch was laid out for display, five-year-old Tanya, who caught the smallest fish, had first choice of the prizes. I was surprised that she chose the bonker. She loved money and chocolate, but now, as a fisherwoman, she had other values. Also, it was the largest of the prizes.

No child returned without a catch. Fish in the waters off Hemming Bay were plentiful. The captains, Vic and Woldy, would have kept close to the shores, where, among the kelp, lurked codfish of all shapes, sizes and colours—all of them hungry for shiny lures. We had a poster in the lodge that had pictures and names of each species, and the children found it satisfying to know just what kind of fish they had caught: a greenling, a ling cod, a yelloweye rockfish or a red snapper. Later that night, before bed, they would record the name and draw the fish in their journals. But first, the fish feast:

### HEMMING BAY FISH AND CHIPS

Be sure to start the day by opening a can of beer, letting it sit to get flat for the batter.

Mix the flat beer with two cups of flour, some salt and an egg.

The wood stove should have been burning, with the vent open, for a couple of hours to ensure there is bubbling hot oil (canola is best) for both the fish and the fries. (Lee and I had left our novels long enough to cut large potatoes into chip-size pieces. We like them with the skin left on.)

It's a pleasure to watch Captain Woldy, now "Master Chef Woldy," drop his carefully skinned fillets into the batter and then into the oil in a large iron frying pan. Listen to them crackle! He turns the pieces over when they are golden brown (about six minutes per side), lays them on newspaper to drain some of the oil, and then pops in more. Meanwhile, the fries are bubbling away in a deeper pot with a wire basket.

Some like their fish and fries with ketchup, some with vinegar, some with tartar sauce (for the fish)—mix together mayo and green hot dog relish—but all agree that these are the best fish and chips in the world!

Besides the fishing derby meal, I have other fond memories of family times at the lodge. We once made a birthday cake for Michael by layering thin pancakes with huckleberries in between. If you whip ice-cold canned milk long and hard enough, it froths up and almost solidifies to serve as icing between the berry layers.

The evening games we played with the children needed no game boards or electronic devices. "Motor Mouth," which required participants to speak non-stop on a subject chosen from a hat, was a particular favourite. There was no need for prizes—laughter was everyone's reward. To my amazement, even our usually taciturn Michael became suddenly loquacious when it was his turn.

## Motor Mouth

Write topics on scraps of paper—lions, ice cream, politics, sports, pets, and so forth. Fold these over and place in a hat.

Have an egg timer handy.

One person at a time pulls out a topic, is given time to read it and think a bit, and then the timer person yells "Go" and flips the four-minute egg timer over.

Each contestant must talk non-stop, with no "ums," for four minutes. If anyone pauses too long or "ums" too much, his or her turn is over.

The children also loved to act out plays they made up themselves—there were no TVs or cellphones at that time in the lodge. Alex, the oldest, was usually the director. All the girls wanted to be maidens in distress, and Michael loved playing the scary villain or a big bad wolf. At Halloween, too, he loved to dress up as something scary—Dracula or Darth Vader. Alex liked to be the rescuer. For their first Halloween together as brothers, Michael dressed up as a dragon, and Alex was the knight in shining armour. (Yes, of course, Tanya was the princess.) Considering that the first six years of Michael's life were very scary—he had been beaten by some of his mother's companions, and he and his sister had often been abandoned—taking on the disguise of a creature who scares others seemed a logical choice.

❧

Sometimes Ron Laidlaw would leave his Serenity Isle to join us for family dinners. On one occasion, he arrived when "Oma," Vic and Woldy's mom, was visiting. After supper we were sitting around a bonfire in what might be called the lodge's backyard, so the kids could roast marshmallows. Ron was getting overly mellow on vodka, and at one point, he simply rolled over on his side to pee on the ground beside him. "Excuse me, Oma," he said. The kids giggled, but Oma got up and left for her bunk bed. From then on, Ron affectionately referred to her as "the old blister," asking us every year how she was doing.

Given this sort of "spontaneous" behaviour, Ron was at times an embarrassment. At other times, he was the friend when in need. When, on our first visit, little Tanya broke out with spots—measles, chicken pox, or maybe mosquito bites?—it was Ron who relieved her of the itching. Even though she was spot-ridden, Tanya still wanted to swim. Ron found us at the swimming rocks and insisted on motoring the child over to his island for a baking soda shower. I went with her, of course, and I was amazed at how quickly Ron got a good fire going in his stove, heating the water and adding the baking soda. I explained that the shower would soothe her itch, and Tanya said, "Okay," though she was clearly apprehensive. Unlike Michael, she always wanted to please. The shy, naked four-year-old stood with her hands covering her private parts in Ron's outdoor shower, which was constructed of cedar poles and a tarp. Ron climbed a ladder behind and poured the soothing mixture from above. I recalled seeing such a shower in *Mogambo*, a film set in Africa; Clark Gable poured water over Ava Gardner. And here we were, on Serenity Isle, re-enacting it!

Our family times together were occasionally marred by conflict, such as when "the boys" (Vic and Woldy) decided we needed a swimming float off our Hemming Lake beach, the beach that was now accessible by boat from the lagoon below the lodge. They set off to build one, saying they'd have it done by dinner. Well, Vic happens to be a master craftsman, and while Woldy might have just roped some logs together, Vic's logs had to be "dapped" (carved out) by chainsaw to receive cross members. The frame was then covered with two-by-eight-foot planks—sought out in old wood piles. The float itself was twenty feet by eight feet, space enough to perform skits or to do a few morning sun salutations. Then, of course, it needed a diving board—another construction challenge. That first day the boys did turn up for dinner, late, but they were absent again on this building project for two more days. Lee and I didn't know it then, but this was a foretelling of much longer absences to come, when the brothers undertook the building of our own lodge. At night, over the sleeping partitions, Lee and I (and the children) could hear each other bawling out our husbands: "This was supposed to be a family holiday!"

When the end project was ready, we all got on the float while Vic and Woldy towed it from the lagoon to the lake. We made it a celebration, tying a Corona beach towel to the end of a pole for a raised flag. Somehow Michael got the privilege of holding it, and, in his usual abstracted way, he swung it about, almost knocking me off the float.

"Goddam it, Michael! Can't you watch what you're doing!" While I swore and the others laughed, Michael put on his look of the Knight of the Sorrowful Countenance, a look he often donned. When I apologized for my outburst, "Sorry, Michael, I'm sure you didn't mean it," I could barely hear his muttered, "Okay."

Despite the bad start, the swimming float and diving board proved a wonderful source of play for the six cousins—and it managed to stay anchored off the beach for thirty years, weathering winter storms and growing, somehow, a fine fern for decoration. Woldy said it made the raft look like a hotel lobby.

When we holidayed in August, the month of meteor showers, we couldn't wait till it was dark, when we would all traipse down to the dock, find a spot to lie down, turn off our flashlights and wait for the heavenly display. "Ahhh!" "Ohhh!" "Did you see that one?" "Quick, look left!" Our shouts of wonder echoed over the lapping sounds of waves.

Some of the children had put rocks in their pockets so that before we left the dark dock, they could throw them in to create star-like glitter in the waters below—the magic of bioluminescence. Their glee at this simple game reminded me of little Alex's pleasure when, years ago, we threw our bucketful of rocks overboard one by one from our sailboat, making *Booms* and creating widening circles.

🪶

But that was summertime, in the growing-up years. Despite our efforts to make our adopted children our own, when they reached fourteen, each of them left our home for the wilderness of the streets.

Our oldest child, Alex, the ornithologist-to-be, died at the age of seventeen in a foolish accident. He and a friend, holidaying at Whistler, climbed a tennis bubble late one night. Alex fell through a weak seam, receiving a head injury, and died on the way to the hospital.

No more holiday fun times. No more fun times ever again, I thought then. How was it possible to lose three children? Friends and relatives couldn't believe it. Woldy and I couldn't believe it. A new wilderness now moved within us.

My writing desk and refuge at Heartstone.

# WRITING FOR SURVIVAL

What sustained me after Alex's sudden death was writing. I had taught composition and poetry at Langara College for over twenty years, but until Alex died, I had rarely written poetry myself.

The night we got our terrible news, delivered at midnight by a teary-eyed young police officer, I kept pounding my husband's chest, repeating, "No, no, no—it can't be true!" I was given a sleeping pill to calm me down. By 3 a.m. I had exhausted myself and fell into a deep slumber. Two lines of poetry woke me the next morning, repeating themselves in my drugged half-consciousness: "He came to us in the dead of winter, / Lighting the darkness with his smile."

My desk was in our bedroom. I had to get to it to write these words down. I was surprised that once I started writing, sixteen lines followed:

He came to us in the dead of winter,
Lighting the darkness with his smile.
He strode through our world,
Giant feet carrying grace.
Roaring down rivers, climbing cliffs,
Drawing, dreaming, kissing, laughing,
His best beloved, a small green bird.

He left us in the dead of winter.
Broken-ribbed, he really couldn't fly.
We mourn him, broken too.

(Alex was born and died in December.)

This poem appeared in print a few days later, on the program for Alex's funeral.

In the grief-ridden days that followed, I continued to write compulsively. My wounded heart's blood was pouring down my arm and becoming ink on paper. Other than that funeral poem, I had no intention of sharing my outpourings—they were simply personal therapy.

I continued teaching college, though now at half time, and I found that my colleagues, fellow English instructors, seemed more open to my sorrow than my family was.

Michael had left home for the streets a few months before Alex died. In my grief, I had no energy to pursue him. But Woldy did. He searched for Michael in the streets and alleys of downtown Vancouver, but he never managed to bring him home for more than a few nights. It was usually Tanya who alerted me in the morning about Michael's empty, unslept-in bed. She even seemed to be satisfied that he had again taken off. Was she envying his independence, his apparent freedom? At that time (the nineties), a kids' drug culture was flourishing in Vancouver. Children as young as fourteen-year-old Michael were leaving home, panhandling during the day, and sharing a "squat" at night, spending their day's earnings on drugs and take-out food. Michael said he felt at home there, remembering, perhaps, his early years before the Ministry for Children had rescued him and his sister.

Immediately after Alex's death, I could only talk to Michael on the phone. Between sobs, I apologized for not being able to see him. I couldn't handle any more pain.

When Alex died, we still had one child at home, Tanya, now aged twelve. As you can imagine, she was not a happy girl. Her adoptive brother had died, her birth brother was living on the streets, and her adoptive parents were absent, too absorbed in our grief. I have learned through discussions with other bereaved parents that surviving siblings feel unloved after the death of a child. The dead child tends to be idealized, and the survivors feel they aren't worthy. Even if they try to assuage their parents' grief, their presence cannot fill the hole left by the departed child. The feelings of being unworthy, of not measuring up to the dead brother or sister, are exacerbated when the child who died was a birth child, and the surviving child was adopted. When we returned home from a day of commemorating Alex, placing a plaque at the river where he loved to kayak, saying praises and singing his favourite songs with a group of his friends, Tanya asked me if I would place a plaque somewhere if she died.

I gasped and fell on my knees to hug her in the chair where she sat. "Oh, don't say you would die too, Tanya!" I sobbed.

Tanya did have suicidal thoughts. The school counsellor who was helping her with her grief alerted us. We found what we thought was a good child psychiatrist, and Tanya continued to see him weekly for the next year or so. Then she too ran away. At age fourteen, she followed her brother to the streets, never actually finding him.

Years later, when Tanya was living on her own, on welfare in a cheap downtown hotel, we met for lunch. I told her I was writing a memoir about the loss of my three children. I asked Tanya if she could tell me why she had left our home.

"I wanted to find out what my birth mother loved more than me," she said, and then she recited a poem she had written about her first heroin overdose:

I hate my life I wanna cry
Maybe laugh or maybe just die
I'm sick and tired of all life's shit
I've reached the bottom of my pit,
I stick a needle in my arm
Thinking it's a magic charm,
And as this high swallows me whole,
I take a look at the world below,
I see me laying on the ground,
Not a movement,
Not a sound,
Heroin.

I got permission from Tanya, who was now in her early twenties, to publish her poem, but when it appeared in my memoir *Snapshots: A Story of Love, Loss, and Life*, Tanya was very angry with me for writing about her street life. To this day, she hasn't forgiven me.

Both Tanya and Michael were children of a drug-addicted mother. Before we adopted them, they had been found wandering the streets of East Vancouver in their pajamas, five-year-old Michael searching through garbage cans in order to feed himself and his little sister. Woldy and I thought that through nurturing them through home cooking, piano and hockey lessons, Girl Guides and wilderness holidays, we could save them. But our grief over the sudden death of Alex incapacitated us as parents just when the children needed us most—at the beginning of their teen years.

I survived the absence of our children with the help of sympathetic friends and compulsive writing. During the first year of my grief over Alex's death, I wrote a poem every day. Everything seemed to have symbolic meaning: a bird, a flower, even a leaf.

And if I didn't write, my depression increased.

Six years later, I searched through my volumes of poems to find those that were most representative of what I now knew about the grief journey after child loss. In attending monthly meetings of The Compassionate Friends (TCF), an international self-help group for bereaved parents, I heard many personal stories. Whether the children were toddlers, teens or even middle-aged at the time of death, and whatever the cause of death, I recognized a commonality in the group sharing. Bereaved parents feel guilty about surviving their children, even if there was no way their actions could have saved them. I remember a father who blamed himself for not being under the tree from which his child fell to her death. If *only* he could have caught her! Depression because of child loss often leads to suicidal thoughts. Partners may feel alienated from each other because they grieve differently, and also because each parent had a different relationship with the child. Though statistics vary, there is a general agreement that the loss of a child can lead parents to divorce. A few months after Alex's death, I asked Woldy why he was no longer crying.

"You're crying enough for the both of us," was his retort.

When I selected the poems I would include in a slim volume tracing my six years of grieving, I kept in mind the feelings common to the bereaved parents I had listened to at monthly TCF meetings. The publishing of *Holding On: Poems for Alex* opened doors for me. Locally, I gave "writing as healing" workshops to other bereaved parents. From these, and from attending monthly Compassionate Friends meetings, I developed some deep and lasting relationships. While friends and relatives who have never lost children hoped I was "getting over" my grief, the mothers I met through TCF understood that we were carrying our wounds for a lifetime. I also presented writing workshops at national and international gatherings of TCF. I travelled as far as Australia with my precious books in a suitcase beside me. I say "precious" because of the books' visual art. My publisher had suggested including photos of Alex and reprints of his drawings. In a poem that includes a reference to an osprey's nest seen at Hemming Bay is Alex's drawing of the nest with the fledglings peeking out. His declaration that seeing this was "the best part" of his holiday attests to the love of nature he gained from his times at Hemming Bay.

## Osprey

### I

A broad-winged bird, cardboard
feathered, each one meticulously
etched, cut out, and glued,

hangs still, suspended
over the empty bed,
its patchwork quilt, neatly

tucked for months now,
its only occupant a Santa-
capped Sylvester, plushly

grinning in black and white,
as if he'd swallowed
the osprey's trout.

### II

Alex's first kayak, handmade
too, was named "Never Sink"
by him, after the

Little Captain's ship in
*Little Captain and Marinka*
(who made great pancakes).

Bought it himself with paper-
route money he collected,
green parrot on his shoulder,
but the maker, Walter,

said the model's trade
name was really "Osprey."

III
In Alex's summer journal,
written three years before
he died, he drew two baby

ospreys peeking from
their spiky nest, sixty feet
above Hemming Lake.

"They were the best part!"
he wrote.

IV
Suk'yu was the name
of the shaman who blessed
Alex's ashes as we fed

them to his favourite river
just before we let the gashed
kayak go—Suk'yu, cleansing

our home with cedar branches,
paused beside the bed,
studying the bird. "My name,"
he said, "means osprey."

There are four other poems in *Holding On* that had Hemming Bay as part of their conception. The cover of the book has a photo of five-year-old Alex and me in profile, Alex playfully pulling away as I hold his wrists to pull him in for a kiss. It was taken on the swimming rocks at Hemming Lake—the rocks where we first met Ron Laidlaw.

But while I composed poems about our wilderness setting, I did not travel there until several summers after Alex's death. The landscape would be empty without him. While my writing pulled me inward, since his son died, Woldy was pulled more and more into the isolation of nature.

Alex's friends, Jonny, Raviv, and Shamus come as volunteer builders.

# BUILDING FOR SURVIVAL

The first time I came to Hemming Bay, I had felt like a stranger, like I didn't belong. After the death of Alex, I felt like a stranger again. Though Woldy continued to go to Hemming Bay with his brother, I couldn't bear to be there, enduring memories of lost happiness. He brought Tanya with him for the first summer of my absence. She was happy to spend time with her three cousins and away from a weeping mom. Now I regret that I didn't go with them. I should have been there for her sake.

Michael was not willing to join his sister and dad. Maybe the thought of being the only boy among four girls put him off, and he seemed to have found his comfort zone on the downtown streets. Once I did manage to find him there, panhandling in front of a McDonald's on Granville Street. We went for a coffee together. When I asked him how he liked living downtown, he said it was "cool." I stupidly offered to bring him a sweater—then we both laughed at my mistake. Soon after that meeting, Michael disappeared from Vancouver's streets. We feared we now had another dead child. But reports of his temporary arrests in US jails assured us that he was at least alive.

The summer after Alex's death, some of Alex's friends went to Hemming Bay with Woldy and Vic. They volunteered to help lay the foundation for our cabin on the personal-use site allotted to us by the community agreement. We had, on past visits, tromped around this piece of forest with our three children, tripping over ferns and salal, looking out at the bay and saying, "This is where we'll put the kitchen," and "Here will be the living room," et cetera. Knowing how far the trek was to Hemming Lake, I no longer argued for a lakefront setting. Back then I didn't quite believe that, like Ron the squatter, we too would—sometime—have a cabin retreat for serenity.

I soon learned that it's not easy building in the wilderness—clearing the land of forest and rocks, and transporting materials by barge, including a generator to keep the power tools going. Equipment breakdowns that required shop repairs meant a four-hour return trip to Campbell River by boat and road. A large supply of groceries had to be hauled in and kept fresh without refrigeration. The crew had to be fed! Housing was no problem—the bunk beds at the communal lodge, with their foam mattresses, were ready and waiting.

Although the land was cleared and the foundations poured in the summers of '93 and '94, construction was put on hold for three years while Vic and Woldy cleared and refreshed their deceased father's house in Yale, BC. "Grandpa George," their father, was an eccentric artist, a taxidermist, a lay preacher and a hoarder. He slept in a tiny clearing among tables laden with tools, art supplies, cameras and bibles. When a table got too full, he would place a piece of plywood on top of the items and again load it with his finds. Once he told me he had a tennis ball for me and would have it for our next visit. (I didn't tell him we usually play with three.) He never did find the ball, but I loved the thought that he wanted to please me. At the end of the first summer of clearing the house's contents, Vic and Woldy advertised the "World's Largest Garage Sale." It amused me that thirteen-year-old Tanya took over selling the multitude of bibles George had collected through the years, bibles in French, Korean, Japanese, Russian, Ukrainian and, yes, many in English. My table at the sale was loaded with junk jewellery, which George had obtained by free mail offers. Woldy undertook to sell the stuffed animals and hides: a fox, a polar bear transformed into a rug, even George's own dead dog, holding a stuffed duck in his jaw. Vic sold the tools, but not all of them—many got boxed up to send to Hemming Bay. Why George needed ten hammers and now Vic did, too, I will never understand. The tool shed that eventually was built behind Heartstone Lodge still holds many of George's possessions. In his later years, Vic confessed that he had inherited his father's hoarding genes.

When the brothers could again turn to their Hemming Bay project, a peculiar circumstance gave the builders something of a head start on the bare bones of construction. Woldy had been teaching at Carson Graham Secondary School, which had an excellent building program. Teachers, and even parents, were invited to submit projects upon which the students could practise their skills. All they had to do was pay for the lumber and submit the plans. We had needed a larger garage for our home in West Vancouver. Our house was an old one, built in 1930, and its moss-covered garage had room for only one car. The plans Woldy handed to the woodwork teacher were ambitious: a two-car garage with a guest room above and an adjacent greenhouse. Unfortunately, Woldy did not apply for a permit to build this large garage complex. Construction had barely started when an inspector came around and shut it down. Our next-door neighbour had blown the whistle on us.

The lumber was all ours now, fitting together like a Lego puzzle. Our home lot was large, so the whole structure was packed up and carefully stacked in our forested yard. There it sat under a tarp for three years.

Growing up in an un-forested farming community, Woldy and Vic had always dreamed of building a fort in the woods. Now, with the help of that school project, their dream was about to be realized, or at least initiated. In the summer of 1998, the brothers assembled a crew to transport the materials for the would-have-been garage and the about-to-be cottage to Hemming Bay. In order to load the lumber onto the truck, they would need to block off one lane of Marine Drive, our home address and the main thoroughfare of West Vancouver. This time Woldy asked for permission, which the police gave, but they specified that we could only do this at midnight, an almost traffic-free period. Lights were set up to illuminate the site. The moving crew included our long-time friend, Brian Murray; Alex's best friend, Jonny Ross; an ex-student of Woldy's, Robert Drygese; an ex-student of mine, Paulus Scholten; and, of course, Woldy and Vic.

The loading project had barely gotten underway when the police arrived. A neighbour across the street had phoned to complain about the lights and the racket—he had to work in the morning and needed sleep. When Woldy explained to the visiting officer that we were instructed to move at midnight, he said he would check the records and talk to the neighbour. This neighbour, as it happened, was not on friendly terms with us. Our dog used to steal his shoes, transporting them across Marine Drive from his back porch to ours. Fortunately, our dog grew out of this puppyhood game before the neighbour carried out his threat to shoot him.

I have a photo that I'm fond of: the crew, finished and exhausted, drinking beer and eating my minestrone soup at two in the morning. I thought the least I could do was contribute nourishment. Needing to wait until six in the morning for the earliest ferry from Horseshoe Bay (West Vancouver) to Departure Bay (Nanaimo on Vancouver Island), the truck driver declined the soup in favour of sleeping time in his truck. By the way, the best minestrone soup I ever had was in Rome, almost half a century ago. This is the closest I have come to duplicating it.

## MINESTRONE SOUP (SERVES AT LEAST 8 HUNGRY WORKERS)

½ lb. salt pork

2 cloves garlic

1 Spanish onion

2 quarts beef stock (made by boiling beef bones for at least an hour)

4 carrots

4 stalks celery

½ small cabbage

4–6 tomatoes

½ lb. green beans

1 large can red kidney beans

4–6 oz. macaroni (6 handfuls)

salt and freshly ground pepper

2 tbsp. chopped parsley

2 tbsp. olive oil

Freshly ground parmesan cheese.

Dice salt pork and sauté in a thick-bottomed soup pot until brown.

Finely chop garlic, cut onion into large chunks, and sauté with pork until golden.

Add beef stock and simmer gently with finely sliced carrots and celery.

Slice cabbage, tomatoes and green beans in fairly large pieces. Add to soup and bring to boil.

Cover and simmer for 90 minutes.

20 minutes before serving, add drained kidney beans and macaroni.

Bring to a boil and simmer until macaroni is tender.

Just before serving, add the parsley, olive oil, salt and pepper.

Sprinkle parmesan cheese over individual servings.

With good bread and cheese, this makes a hearty meal.

⚓

From Nanaimo, our load would travel north for a couple of hours, pulling into Marine Link Transportation, north of Campbell River, where it would then be lifted onto a barge and towed to Hemming Bay. Marine Link is a key link indeed to the settlements north of Campbell River in the inner waters of the Gulf of Georgia (within the area now called the Salish Sea). Since there are no ferries or other means of public transport to remote villages or settlements such as ours, Marine Link operates as a tourist transport as well as a supplier of goods and equipment. What follows is my brother-in-law's description of the first step toward creating the dream cabin, including the landing of our jigsaw house, and more. A longer version has been published in *Pushing the Beach: The Story of Marine Link Transportation and the MV Aurora Explorer*, by Alan H. Meadows with S.C. Heal.

It was with great anticipation and excitement that Woldy and I stood on the beach of our wilderness property at Hemming Bay, East Thurlow Island, awaiting the arrival of Marine Link's delivery. It was mid-July 1998. Rounding Brougham Point, still a mere speck on the horizon, was the *Aurora Explorer*. We could hear the steady, high-pitched drone of her twin diesels.

Woldy and I, along with several helpers and friends of Alex's, had spent the last four days in Marine Link's staging yard, organizing and packaging the contents of a sixty-foot semi-trailer, a flat-deck truck and a large single-axle moving van into thirty-three totes (four-by-four-foot to four-by-eight-foot shipping containers, built on-site). The shipment consisted of years of doors, windows and memorabilia recycled from my building jobs; building materials and hardware from our father's estate; bricks, cement and mortar for a four-flue chimney; lifts of plywood and new lumber; plus a prefab, eighteen-hundred-square-foot building in packable sections. As the *Aurora* neared the beach, we could hear the chatter of the bridge deck radio and the mate on the bow giving instructions to the skipper as they made a safe landing. When the ramp came down, the ship's crew fired up forklifts and cranes, and orders were yelled above the roar of machinery. The invasion had begun. It felt like D-day at Omaha Beach.

The first half-dozen loads went like clockwork. Then, a half-hour into the operation, on its way back for another load, the forklift suddenly stopped. Alvin, the driver, tried to restart the machine several times, but to no avail. "Well, isn't that a nice howdy-do. I guess we'll have to change the fuel filter. No problem. We always keep a spare taped to the steering column under the dash." Upon inspection, he came back scratching his head. The last guy who changed the filter didn't replace it.

"Do you have a five-gallon bucket, a piece of half-inch hose and a hose clamp? We're gonna set up a direct siphon and bypass the filter." Bucket, hose and hose clamp were supplied. "Next, we'll have to secure the bucket to the cab roof." Bungies and rope were fetched. After that, he removed the filter mounted on the engine, placed one end of the hose into the bucket on the cab roof, securing it with some tape so it wouldn't fall out once the siphon was set up. Then, putting the other hose end into his mouth, he began to suck out a mouthful of diesel fuel. The hose end was pinched and then clamped directly to the fuel pump. Now, all was ready for priming. In order to do this, each one of the four injectors had to be taken off individually, hand-pumped via the hand primer pump until fuel squirted out, and quickly screwed back in so as not to get any air into the system. Diesel was squirting and dripping everywhere.

Climbing back into the cab, Alvin said, "She should go now." He hit the start button and the diesel sprang to life. Thumbs-up and we were back in business!

Vic goes on to describe how load after load was now forklifted to the beach.

Some readers will appreciate the ingenuity of the repair of the broken fuel filter as described in such enthusiastic detail by Vic. Myself, although I can applaud Alvin's creativity (and Vic's description of it), I could not imagine doing any such repair. As a less-handy female, I felt left out of this building project. When I finally returned to Hemming Bay with the brothers and their volunteer crew, instead of staying at the community lodge with them, I opted to sleep alone on our comfortable motorsailer. Woldy and I had purchased a larger boat after the children left us and we sold our home in West Vancouver, with its three empty children's bedrooms. Besides being away for periods during the summer, either at Hemming Bay or Yale, during the school year Woldy was often away leading camping trips in his role as principal of an alternative high school. Though I was still teaching college and had my writing desk with a view in our upstairs bedroom, echoes of the missing children in the big empty house depressed me. We moved to a smaller home in West Van and took our newly purchased thirty-foot motorsailer, the *Youngster*, to Hemming Bay. This was time consuming, involving two days of travel; Woldy would have rather spent that time working with his brother.

As much as I loved the solitude of my floating writing studio in the time I stayed aboard the *Youngster* anchored in Hemming Bay, I felt spoiled and useless, listening to the sounds of the labouring men behind the shoreline trees. I did make sandwiches on board and rowed them ashore at what I thought was lunchtime (noonish). But the building crew, under the guidance of the work-obsessed brothers, would not take their break until around two. Again, Woldy's and my concepts of time were at odds. After that trip, and for a number of years, I absented myself from the wilderness. During the summer weeks of separation, while Woldy was building, I was playing tennis, lunching with friends (other bereaved mothers, other writers), writing poetry and wondering how he was doing—there was no phone link to the building site. If I received any news from or about Tanya or Michael, I was desperate to share it with him, but it had to wait till he was off island, at least back in Campbell River, before we could talk.

Despite the hard labour and mishaps, Woldy and Vic became more and more enthusiastic about the challenge of building a home in the woods. They could only spend a few weeks each summer on this labour (Vic had his own construction company to run at home), so when they were on-site, they worked from dawn to dusk. The boys who accompanied them—Alex's friends—described their time there as being at the "Sosnowsky Gulag." I enjoyed hearing these stories when Woldy returned, but I also resented his absence and the expenses involved: building materials and tools, transportation, feeding the crew. And the progress seemed to drag along so slowly. I actually wanted Woldy to abandon the project, to spend more time with me exploring inland waters and islands on our boat. I had taken up a new part-time vocation in writing destination articles for *Pacific Yachting* and was incapable of making these long boating journeys by myself. I thought of M. Wylie Blanchet, author of the bestselling *The Curve of Time*, who, after her husband's death, spent long summers with her five small children on a twenty-five-foot sailboat. I thought of Kate Braid, also a writer, who was capable of swinging a hammer with the strongest of men, and I felt inadequate.

For Woldy, the building of Heartstone was a tribute to our son Alex. Shortly after his death, we had attended a Kriya breathing workshop, led by a cousin of Woldy's. We had never been interested in meditation before, but we trusted Woldy's cousin's leadership and were desperate for any help during our deep grief. Woldy and I lay side by side on mats on a church basement floor. I could hear him breathing beside me, deeply, and more deeply. Suddenly his breathing turned to sobs—loud, wracking sobs. I wanted to turn to him, to embrace him, to comfort him, but I knew that the initiates, the "breathers," were supposed to be on their own journey. It wasn't until much later that Woldy shared with me the vision that the Kriya experience had revealed, releasing at last his deepest pain:

I was sitting on the rock outcropping in front of our chosen building site on the shore of Hemming Bay. From my position, I could see the muddy beach exposed from the retreating tide. Alex appeared on the beach and bent his long, lean frame over to pick up a bag of cement that had somehow landed there. Waves of light played over his back, giving the image that each backbone itself was quivering. Gradually, knobs appeared on his back, as if they were growing from it. In shimmering light, these knobs grew into horns, the horns of a stag.

When Woldy shared this vision with Vic, they both agreed on its message. They needed to build. They needed to erect a structure in Alex's memory.

"Building for survival" was Woldy's recipe for coping with grief. My recipe was writing and travelling to present at Compassionate Friends conferences. Sometimes Woldy would accompany me, but he would always rather be at Hemming Bay. Working in the silence of the surrounding forest, Woldy felt close to his son. Sometimes, after he shared his experiences and feelings with me, I would try to capture them in a poem:

Robert, one of Woldy's ex-students, helping to clear our site.

Woldy pouring cement with the help of Alex's friends.

## Raven Talks to Woldy

Smelling of musk oil and sweat,
he swings the pick into the rockbound
earth. Alone. The forest echoes.

But wait . . . there's someone talking,
    someone squawking:
        right on, Dad!
        squawk   squawk
        keep swinging, Dad!
        squawk  squawk
        I'm watching, Dad!
        squawk  squawk
        black wings shining, Dad
        squawk  squawk

        watch me flying, Dad.

Woldy always came home from the wilderness radiating exuberance and smelling of diesel oil, musk, wood smoke and cedar. As he stepped through the door, he reminded me of Alex coming in from his first full day of whitewater kayaking—smelling of water and sunshine, glowing, and saying, "I've just had the best day of my life!" In both cases, I thought, *Without me!*

The framing and construction begins.

# HEARTSTONE EMERGES

In the summers before the big transport of building materials, Woldy, Vic and three of Alex's friends prepared our site for construction. Vic and Woldy are heavy-set Ukrainian men, used to working with their large hands and strong bodies. They actually love physical work and are famous for helping friends move—in one case, they hoisted a large antique wardrobe through an upstairs window after the professional movers had declared it was impossible to get it up the stairs. Jonny, Joff and Raviv were athletic young men, but they were city boys, not used to hard outdoor labour. Their physical activities had been sports at high school; their jobs had been as dish pigs and then waiters in local restaurants. Now they were college or university students and did not get much chance to exercise. Clearing the wilderness lot meant felling trees, cutting underbrush and digging up tree roots and boulders to excavate for foundation footings—fun for a few hours, maybe, especially while kibitzing with their buddies, but labouring from daylight to dusk proved taxing for them. After they returned to their city lives, after decrying their time at the "Sosnowsky Gulag," their muscles recovered, and their bruises and cuts healed. Their bodies suffered no permanent damage, but the boys left a permanent imprint on our forest dwelling, gouging their initials, and Alex's, into its cement footings.

What continued to inspire the crew, besides their love for their dead friend and the feeling of being close to nature, was the

Ukrainian-sized portions they were served by Woldy, accompanied by toasts of vodka and several beers. Their favourite meal, Jonny told me, was "Logger's Steak," a recipe that Woldy had learned from his logging days—when he too had a youthful appetite.

## LOGGER'S STEAK

1 large flank or round steak

oil

butter

onion

mushrooms

2 beef Oxo cubes (or beef-in-a-mug)

1 bunch of parsley

3 or more cloves of garlic

a handful of flour

salt and pepper


Braise steak in oil and butter (on both sides) over high heat. Remove steak from pan and set aside.

Fry onions and mushrooms till tender.

Sprinkle flour over everything.

Mix 2 cups of water with 2 bouillon cubes and garlic, and add to pan.

Allow to thicken slightly. Add another ½ cup of water or wine.

Add steak and reduce heat.

Simmer for at least 90 minutes.

Serve with mashed potatoes and boiled carrots.

If you have bread, use it to soak up the gravy. If you
have fresh greens, make a salad.

For Alex's friends, the call of the wild was eventually silenced by
the need to work for college fees, and the volunteer crew disappeared. Vic and Woldy then hired a paid worker, Robert, who had
been Woldy's student when he was principal of Keith Lynn Alternative School. Robert was even sturdier than the Ukrainian brothers. Members of his northern tribe, the Dogrib, are known for
their stocky build and strong physique. Robert measured about
five foot seven and had a girth to suit a taller man. If he weren't so
strong, you might have said he was fat. But flab could never move
what Robert could. He moved rocks the size of giant seals—and
liked doing it! Woldy and Vic called him "the human backhoe."

Sometimes strong workers arrived unexpectedly. Our former
boat partners, Tom and Jenny Bowen, were cruising the inland
waters on a friend's yacht. Before our family outgrew our twenty-six-foot sailboat, the Bowens had been shared owners, taking
turns to cruise and to clean. Tom and Jenny knew that Woldy and
Vic would be at their building site and that Hemming Bay was a
safe anchorage. Just when extra hands and muscles were needed to raise a central beam, Tom and Jenny appeared from up the
beach path and were immediately put to work. Well, not Jenny,
who is about five foot five, but Tom, at six foot three, was just the
right height to hold up the huge beam while Vic hammered it in
place. Now the builders were ready to place the floor joists for the
second storey.

Other workers—strangers—arrived from time to time. As per
the co-operative's agreement, Vic and Woldy were building at least
fifty feet from the shore, leaving trees in between to maintain a

wilderness appearance. But although their building project could not be seen by passing boaters, its construction could certainly be heard by any who chose to overnight in the once quiet bay. Anchored off a favourite cliff that Woldy and I had used as sanctuary when we first arrived at Hemming Bay, a Seattle couple, John and Julie, decided to find the source of the sounds of hammers, drills and axes. Tying their rowboat at the base of the rock headland in front of our site, they cautiously approached the builders. Vic and Woldy were pleased to welcome the visitors; it was a chance to pause and chat and to show off their project. John and Julie were fascinated by the idea of this wilderness home and invited the brothers aboard their forty-foot power cruiser for a spaghetti dinner that night. The next morning, they showed up early with work gloves, ready to help.

Showing the newcomers the layout of the now-framed structure, Woldy told them of a plan for a large fireplace, made of stones to be collected from the nearby beaches. "Ah, we collect stones," said Julie. "Heart-shaped stones." A year later, when Vic and Woldy approached the headland sheltering their building site, they noticed a large heart-shaped rock sitting on the moss in a cleft, a gift, they guessed, from their new friends. Later, it was to become the focal point of the floor-to-ceiling fireplace, inspiring the dwelling's name, "Heartstone Lodge."

The brothers wanted their fireplace to reflect the natural environment, and they had scouted the neighbouring shores for good-sized rocks to add to John and Julie's founding stone. It was four years into the construction when Vic contacted Rod Gordon, a professional mason whom he had used on city construction jobs. For a foolproof fireplace, one that could heat a two-storey house without burning down the surrounding forest, an expert was needed.

Woldy described Rod to me as tall, slim, muscular and well

able to carry an eighty-pound bag of cement on one shoulder while climbing up the hill from the beach. The brothers hired him to spend four days in the wilderness, not only to put together a fireplace, but also to build a wall for a dam on the creek above Heartstone. I remember Woldy coming home from observing Rob at work, saying that he was like a dancer, moving from stone to stone, cementing each chosen one in place with just the right amount of mortar. The fireplace was to have four chimneys, one for the open fire in the living room, one for the cooking stove, one for the airtight heater downstairs and one for a smaller heater upstairs. Despite his brief stay, Ron still managed to escape for a couple of hours to go fly fishing on Hemming Lake. He came back with four good-sized trout. Songs have been written about loggers and fishermen, and I think Woldy could compose a song about this mason, who joked and chatted while he worked.

The fireplace was a core necessity to make Heartstone liveable. Another major project was needed to make it easily accessible—a three-hundred-foot dock that reached out to a moor-able depth, even at low tide. The building of this dock complex (five small docks linked by bolts and chains) took three summer seasons of intense labour. Lengthy logs had to be salvaged from surrounding beaches. One ready-made but crude dock was found almost intact on the shore of a nearby island. Woldy and Vic waited for a high tide to pry it loose, tied it to their skiff and towed it back across the channel to Heartstone's beach.

Another ready-made dock was acquired by trade. The brothers discovered it at Oleo's floating restaurant in Frederick Arm (just ten miles north of Hemming Bay). Oleo's, which was owned by Paul Montoya, the son of founder and cook Leo, was in danger of sinking. Paul asked Vic and Woldy to procure twenty-eight barrels to prop it up. They could have his extra dock in return. Vic and Woldy found a chicken production operation in the Fraser Valley, where they paid three hundred dollars for twenty-eight plastic barrels that had contained the cod liver oil needed to replace the vitamins that chickens raised in artificial light were missing. For months, Vic's van, which was used to pack the barrels to the site, stank of cod liver oil. Paul transported the barrels by sea to the restaurant, and Vic and Woldy towed "home" a sturdy sixty-foot dock.

One could find Oleo's restaurant listed in sailing atlases, but mostly its visitors were summer sailors who exchanged stories while rowing between their anchored boats in various bays of BC's popular inland waters. "Have you been to Oleo's in Frederick Arm? You can tie up overnight and enjoy a meal of stuffed peppers, cabbage rolls, roasted duck or chicken, followed by a huge piece of moist chocolate cake. All for twenty dollars a person. Bring your own wine." On my occasional visits to Hemming Bay, when Woldy and I had made a compromise—a couple of weeks exploring on the *Youngster*, and a couple of weeks with me afloat in the bay while he worked ashore—I was able to talk Woldy into taking an afternoon and evening off from the building project to spend a night at Oleo's. Sitting at a slightly rocking, linen-covered table surrounded by the burgundy, embossed-brocade wallpaper and lace curtains, listening to Leo's tales of visiting bears and winter storms, we knew this was an experience never to be found anywhere else in the world. Before returning to our boat to sleep, we ordered fresh baked bread and the best cinnamon buns on the coast, baked by Leo's wife, Ruth, and delivered to our boat the next morning by their daughter, Katerina. Sometimes other members of the Hemming Bay Community who were also boat owners would join us for a night at Leo's.

When I heard that Ruth and Leo had lost a son in a boating accident and that, since his death, Ruth had never appeared outside the kitchen, I gave a copy of my collection of grief poems to Katerina to give to her mother. When we moored at Leo's the next year, Ruth came on board to visit us. Grief can be a powerful unifier, bridging gaps of age and experience. The cook on a remote floating restaurant and the city college instructor had no problem communicating.

Why were there no fish or shellfish dishes served on this restaurant at sea? Well, Leo knew that the boaters who ventured this far north to visit him had already had their fill of salmon, cod, crab and prawns. Once Woldy and I had pulled up such a load of prawns in our overnight trap that we ate prawns for three days in a row: barbecued prawns dipped in garlic butter one night, prawns in a tomato sauce on spaghetti the next, and curried prawns on rice the final night. After we had finally eaten that load, I longed for the simplicity of my standby corned-beef-out-of-a-can meal.

STANDBY CORNED BEEF HASH

1 can corned beef

1 can niblets corn

a couple of potatoes (boiled first)

green pepper

cooking onion

2 eggs (or as many as you have eaters)

Fry the vegetables and corned beef in saved bacon fat.

Crack eggs over top.

Cover to desired doneness.

Delicious with ketchup!

Likewise, when we visited Leo's, we were pleased have a break from our usual fish or seafood dinners. And the fresh bread and chocolate cake were prized by all visiting boaters.

⚘

On one of my visits to Hemming Bay, I was able to observe Woldy and Vic installing the "billets" they had built to float the docks—two-by-eight-by-four-foot plywood boxes that were then filled with Styrofoam. How two farm-raised boys figured all this out baffles me. But they did. Now, years later, you can amble down from Heartstone; walk the three hundred feet of sturdy floating dock, carrying a book and a folding chair; and sit and read in the sun, disturbed only by the splashing of dolphins on their afternoon fishing trips, the occasional screech of an eagle and the frequent chatter of kingfishers as they dive from high overhanging branches. You could even bring a journal with you and write!

Hand-building the 300-foot dock.

The community lodge was a welcome shelter for all.

# Encounters with Nature

Though I wasn't present for most of the building endeavor, and I resented the time and money poured into it, I couldn't help but admire Woldy and Vic's hard labour, ingenuity and devotion to their project. Woldy kept telling me I would love being at Hemming Bay once our own lodge was finished. But it never seemed to be finished. It was the summer of 1993 when they first cleared the site. Twelve years later, Heartstone was still not habitable. I remembered how Penelope, wife of Odysseus, secretly unravelled her weaving at night because, in the absence of her husband, she had promised to marry another once her tapestry was completed. Odysseus took ten years to get home from the Trojan War. I told friends that I thought "the boys" were prolonging their construction because, once all the doors and windows were in place, their wives might arrive to do some interior decorating, turning their "man cave" into a women's retreat.

Meanwhile, like Penelope, I mostly waited at home. I didn't long to be in the wilderness with Woldy, but I did love hearing his wilderness tales when he returned. Some of the stories were funny, some scary, and some sad.

Even before they started working on their own building site, Vic and Woldy would sometimes go to Hemming Bay to help on some communal project. One summer they rebuilt a bridge over a creek that interrupted the road to the Hemming Bay Lodge. Woldy returned from that trip to tell me of the death of Buster

Brown, our squatter's dog, the one that Alex had fallen in love with on our first-ever visit to Hemming Bay. Ron had left Buster alone on Serenity Isle when he took a trip for groceries with a friend who had a seaplane. As the plane banked to land, Ron and the pilot saw a circle of wolves surrounding Buster, taking turns lunging at him. By the time the men had docked, the wolves had scattered, carrying away chunks of flesh and leaving behind Buster Brown's torn corpse and Ron's broken heart. Visiting Ron's empty cabin on another trip to Hemming Bay, Woldy snapped a photo of Buster Brown's gravesite. White capital letters cut into a cedar slab held Ron's tribute to his beloved dog:

BUSTER BROWN BOW
A SMALL BROWN DOG AGED 6½ YEARS
MY TRUE PARTNER, SEPT. 4, 1974 – APRIL 19, 1981
KILLED BY WOLVES AT HOME. OUR HOUSE IS
NOW EMPTY. MY SORROW IS TOO GREAT.

Ron Laidlaw, April 26, 1981

Ron did not leave his island immediately after losing Buster. It was a bureaucratic attack that made him leave. At least that's how Ron saw the BC government's move to register all Crown land occupied by squatters and to charge the occupants back taxes. Ron could not come up with the twelve hundred dollars he was billed for his years of residing on his island. In any case, he felt that being registered in this way inhibited his freedom—his island no longer seemed serene. He left behind his well-built cabin, his nine bean rows, his outdoor shower and his tribute to Buster Brown.

We knew that wolves were good swimmers, able to reach our East Thurlow Island from Vancouver Island or other surrounding habitats, but I was surprised to learn that cougars could swim long distances too.

One day, Arno and Jenny, who had recently bought one of the for-sale shares in the Hemming Bay Community, were returning to the main lodge after kayaking on the lake. The couple were experienced outdoor people, having kayaked through the turbulent waters of Johnstone Strait to reach East Thurlow Island, and having chosen to camp outdoors rather than build on their own "personal use space" or stay in the communal lodge. This day, as they were approaching the lodge to visit with the caretaker, Arno in front on the narrow trail, Jenny behind, the island's quiet was pierced by Jenny's screams. Arno turned to see his wife on the ground, a young cougar pawing her head. He went after the cat with his kayak paddle and managed to frighten him away. Carrying his bleeding wife to the lodge, he was thankful to find the caretaker in and ready to phone for an emergency helicopter. Jenny was flown to the Campbell River hospital, given a blood transfusion and a morphine drip, and emergency room doctors sewed together her ripped-open skull.

I was horrified by this tale. My *National Geographic* view of benevolent Nature was shattered; the news that wildlife officers had successfully trapped and killed the offending cougar was equally disturbing. At least, I thought, there was a phone connection in the community lodge—Heartstone, down a long trail and across the bay, had no phone signal.

A few years after this incident, when Arno and Jenny had joined us for dinner (in the now functioning Heartstone Lodge), I asked Jenny how it had affected her.

"How were you ever able to return here after such a traumatizing attack?"

"Well, I wasn't really traumatized," replied Jenny. "The cougar, after all, had no vicious intent. It wasn't like an attack by a thug in the city. It was just hungry."

Jenny did admit that she and Arno no longer camped outdoors.

They gave up their sense of freedom in the wild in favour of the safety of the sturdily built community lodge.

An interesting footnote to this cougar story occurred a couple of years later when a stray Abyssinian kitten, looking very cougar-like, wandered into Arno and Jenny's yard, begging to be adopted. They report that of all their pets, this one has been the most affectionate. Did he come to apologize for his species, they wondered?

✴

On one of Woldy and Vic's spring building trips to Heartstone, they, too, had an unpleasant encounter with nature. When they left Heartstone in the late fall, they always boarded it up well, fastening plywood over the doors and windows. But when they unsealed the first door upon their return the following spring, they were met with a putrid odour. Once boards had been removed from the windows, letting in the light, they could see that an uninvited visitor had taken advantage of their winter absence. White and green mold, interspersed with feces, covered all surfaces—kitchen counters, tables, beds, the floor, everywhere. Ripped-open bags of flour, sugar, oatmeal and rice were scattered all over the place. Examining the feces, which were comparable in size to that of a small dog, the men decided it could only have been a martin.

Fortunately, there was bleach on hand, and buckets, and scrub brushes, and lots of water. Vic and Woldy had brought two friends with them, intending to spend the three-day May long weekend building and moving docks. Instead, it took the four men two full days of scrubbing to make Heartstone habitable for humans again.

This home invasion was of course a source of frustration—time spent at Heartstone was precious and meant to be devoted to construction. But by the time Woldy returned to tell me the tale, it had turned into an amusing story of man's helplessness before the omnipotence of Nature.

Once the sun has gone down, telling stories is a prime occupation at either Heartstone or the community lodge. Once Heartstone became a functioning dwelling—with fireplace, cookstove and running water, Vic and Woldy loved entertaining any visiting Hemming Bay Community members, or even anchored boaters, at our large kitchen table. In the over forty years since the formation of our wilderness co-op, only four out of the twenty shareholders had built their own cabins on the island. I mentioned in an earlier chapter the construction by a fly-in crew of the Wakefields' cabin on the lagoon. Another couple managed to get away with barging in a camping trailer, and by covering it with cedar shingles, they blended it in with the woods. Yet another pair hired our caretaker and his friend, an oyster farmer, to build their wilderness home. Terry and Fred built it from salvaged cedar with a chainsaw mill. The Carlsons built a substantial shed, but in the process, Bob Carlson fell and broke his arm so badly that all construction stopped. So the 232 acres of East Thurlow Island owned by our community remained the wilderness it was intended to stay. Visiting boaters who anchored in Hemming Bay were alerted by modest signs that this was private property (and so should be respected), but they would not see any noticeable dwellings if they decided to take a walk in the woods. If they made it as far as the community lodge, the caretaker would let them know that they should not use the lake as a bathtub. Their soap and shampoo would contaminate the community's drinking water.

Members who chose not to build continued to book time in the community lodge. If a number of members were staying and others were holidaying in their cabins, communal dinners would be held. At these dinners would be a combination of original founding members and new members who had bought from shareholders who had found the wilderness not really to their liking. Once, when participating in one of these dinners, I was pleased to hear a long tale from Bob Samson.

From our first encounter with the Hemming Bay Community, I remembered Bob as an impressive presence. An attractive man with dark hair and a short dark beard, Bob had warm eyes that invited no frivolity, but also made no judgement. A man you could trust. His engineering expertise had made the main lodge a place where you could take a shower or read a book at night. Now, thirty years later, behind a white beard, Bob's quiet presence still invited respect.

Arriving with our dinner contribution of clam chowder, I found a seat on the lodge's large deck beside Suzi Wakefield, a long-time member and a woman with interesting pursuits—she had formerly been a trainer of counsellors in Washington public schools and was now a professional photographer. I wanted to catch up on her life after a year's absence, but when I tried to start a conversation, she said, "Shh! Bob's telling a story."

I fell silent among the twelve listeners who were holding their glasses of wine or bottles of beer, not wanting to miss a sentence while sipping. Bob was recounting the organizing of kayaking equipment and food supplies, the arrangement of visas and the flight to Alaska, and he was now telling of the arduous crossing of the Bering Strait from Nome, Alaska, to the outermost shores of Russia. The three kayakers, Bob Sampson, Tim Kennedy and Dave Carlson (also a Hemming Bay member), had been training for months for this expedition. They had researched the waters and reviewed reports of the two kayakers who had managed this challenge before them. They expected to be away from their Seattle homes for several weeks and had prepared their families for their absence. Part of Bob's tale described the sea journey on the straits, paddling thirty-two miles on their first day, then through six-foot swells on their second. He described passing through floating chunks of icebergs and delaying their shore landings when they sighted roaming polar bears.

Amazing! But not nearly as amazing as what happened when they finally landed on Russian soil. Instead of being greeted as intrepid explorers, they were arrested as alien invaders. Their kayaks were confiscated, and they found themselves housebound prisoners in the town of Uelen. As such, they were welcomed and dined, but after ten days without contact with home or permission to continue their journey, their anxiety grew. This occurred in July 1994, well after the "fall" of the Soviet Union. But the power of bureaucracy and the habit of officials engaging in corruption, or "Blat," persisted.

Listening to Bob's story of temporary imprisonment, my mind wandered to the journey that Woldy, Alex and I had taken into the Soviet Union in 1979. Alex had been almost four years old when we travelled by Volkswagen van through the Iron Curtain countries of Hungary and Bulgaria to visit Woldy's relatives in the Ukraine. Our visas allowed us to stay in campgrounds along the way, specified and paid for ahead of time. When we were entering the Soviet Union proper, attempting to reach relatives in Odessa, we were detained for six hours. Woldy and I were questioned separately to make sure our stories were consistent. Little Alex, meanwhile, played with his dinosaur collection, to the fascination of the guards. Our female translator (Woldy had to pretend that he didn't speak Russian, as our Visas did not allow us to visit relatives) was enchanted by the boy and kept pleading with the guards to let us go. We finally made it to the relatives in Odessa, but always under close surveillance.

Bob, Tim and Dave did get their kayaks back, after a heavy fine for landing on Russian soil without the correct documents, and they flew back to Seattle to the arms of their worried spouses. The group of listeners on the communal deck sighed a communal sigh of relief and resumed drinking their beer or wine.

I was still a bit distracted, absorbed by my own memories. Alex had also been a kayaker. What he liked at sixteen was the danger of whitewater kayaking on rivers. Had he lived, would he too have ventured out to kayak the dangers of such waters as the Bering Strait? I remembered how we had let him cross the treacherous waters of Johnstone Strait on one of our summer journeys to Hemming Bay. Woldy, Vic, Michael, Tanya and I had left from Rock Bay in our runabout boat with our week's supply of food, crossing at fifteen kilometres per hour, which usually took twenty-five minutes. Alex had brought his kayak on our VW van's roof, and he wanted to cross on his own. Woldy said we should let him. I lost the argument.

Once ashore at Hemming Bay, we could no longer see the lone kayaker around the headland. When would he appear again? After helping to schlep our supplies up to the communal lodge, I went back down to the shore to wait. And wait. And wait. How could we have allowed this? A sixteen-year-old alone on a dangerous sea? Would Alex even recognize the turn into Hemming Bay? Hours passed. Two hours, I think, but it seemed longer.

Finally, he appeared and landed!

"Mom, I almost drowned!" he shouted, as if proud of the fact. "The whales almost tipped me!"

"Whales?"

"Yes, a whole pod of them! They were so beautiful—but scary!"

My brave boy was right to be scared. Killer whales that swim off our coast have been known to tip small vessels, presumably in play. Years earlier, Woldy and I had been crossing the Georgia Strait in our first sailboat, a twenty-footer, and we were hypnotized as a black metallic fin came broadside towards us. I thought it was a submarine! We held our breath. The apparent predator simply ducked under and came up on the other side of our vessel. Just having fun.

After Alex had caught his breath, he told me how exciting it was to be surrounded by dipping fins, then how frightening. But here he was, telling the tale, and showing me a big open blister on his thumb from two hours of paddling. When he died six months later, he still had that scar.

Alex and I joined the others at the lodge, to much excitement and acclaim. That is, acclaim from Vic and Woldy and Alex's cousins. Michael scowled, and Tanya ignored the fuss. Again, Michael's older brother had achieved something that felt out of his reach. Alex spent his first summer as a baby aboard our small sailboat; I have photos of him jolly-jumping from the boom. So, he had a natural affinity for the movement of water. When we adopted Tanya and Michael at four and six years old, they could not swim, ride a bike or catch a ball. No one had played with them or taught them these skills, which many think come naturally to all children. Michael did prove to be a good hockey player, and Woldy even became the coach of his team. Alex didn't like team sports but sometimes went along to cheer at Michael's games. Tanya, too, took to the ice, becoming a competitive figure skater at age twelve.

## CLAM CHOWDER

(Our contribution to the communal dinner.) Clam digging—like playing in the mud—is an activity all our children liked. At Hemming Bay, when the tide is out, it's fun to dig for clams in the mucky, mud-like sand. Wherever you are, though, pay attention to the government's red-tide warnings.

Start digging where you see squirts of water erupting from holes in the sand. Keep the little spherical shells, and throw out the flat, soft shells. Keep them in a bucket of sea water for a few hours to let them clean themselves.

Boil them in fresh water till they open (about 10 minutes). *Save the broth* when you drain them!

Separate the clams from their shells. Keep the shells in a bucket and the clams in a bowl, and set both aside.

Fry some chopped bacon in a big soup pot.

Fry chopped onions, green pepper, garlic, carrots, celery and chunks of potato in the bacon fat.

Add the broth you saved, and then the clams.

Add a can of diced tomatoes.

Flavour with salt, pepper, parsley.

Serve with thick slices of French bread.

Return the clamshells to the sea. If you throw them back at night, you can observe the magic of bioluminescence as the sinking shells cause small plankton to sparkle.

Baby Alex jolly-jumping on the boom.

The grandchildren rehearse "Dumb Ways to Die."

# DEPARTURES AND ARRIVALS

On a recent visit to Hemming Bay, I began writing this manuscript. I had to. Vic and Woldy had proudly shown me my writing desk in Heartstone's upstairs master bedroom, under a window looking out on giant firs. They had even placed a cushion on the wooden desk chair, inviting me to write for hours. The window frame still awaited finishing, but the room itself had a pleasant cottagey feel with the four-inch tongue-and-groove V-joints of the vaulted ceiling, painted white. Unlike the open plan of the communal lodge, Heartstone's walls reached the ceiling, and our bedroom actually had a door to it. This was a good thing, as at night, rather than stumbling to the outhouse, we pee in a bucket. Woldy's and my first queen-size bed, from when we downsized from a house to an apartment, was now a feature, with its comfy mattress and down quilt. Many pieces of our furniture had moved from the city to the wilderness. We had always favoured antiques, and the old pieces seemed quite at home in a rustic forest dwelling. And now that the house was almost finished, I had jobs to do—washing windows, painting walls. I, too, was feeling at home.

My writing project was formidable: How to document and describe forty-two years of Hemming Bay Community history—what to include? What to leave out? As I write this chapter, I'm aware of the imposing presences left by those who have died.

✦

A woman I remember well, even though we only met for one night each time over the years, was Marty. She was the partner of Dick Wright, a man of some means who flew his float plane when he came to stay in his shingle-covered caravan. When I had first met Dick, early in the community's inception, he had what is sometimes called an "arm-piece" wife—blond, full bosomed (with cleavage), and wearing heavy makeup. She didn't last long as a partner in the wilderness, though I don't know if that was an element in their divorce. The next time I met Dick, he had Marty with him, a woman with no pretence to beauty, but one who radiated energy. One could find Marty transporting wheelbarrows full of rocks to mend the potholed road from the bay to the lodge (only navigable by a six-wheeled Gator, a utility vehicle the community eventually purchased to facilitate the unloading of week-long supplies of groceries and gear).

Over the years, Marty and Dick would make the trip from their shingled caravan to the Heartstone building site to check on its progress. This involved trekking down the old logging road and rowing across the bay. They always brought their secret mixture of Kahlua, vodka and "?" (their secret ingredient) in a large plastic Coke bottle. Once Heartstone was open for company, they joined us for a fish dinner, telling tales of their first meeting at a nudist camp.

Marty wanted to marry and thought that the ceremony could be held on Heartstone's extensive docks. Our granddaughter, Ainsley, the baby Tanya had had on her own, was now ten and staying with us. She got busy designing Marty's wedding dress and making up a wedding-feast menu. The couple ended up having their ceremony in Hawaii, not Hemming Bay. They married shortly before Marty died of internal complications. Suffering from Parkinson's, Dick soon followed her.

❦

The community lodge needed a year-long caretaker to ensure its preservation and to keep an eye on the other dwellings and the forest itself. The history of Hemming Bay Community caretakers is an interesting one, beginning with Charlie and Perky Martoff—young, newly married artists. They lasted for one year, living through the winter under layers of sweaters, being spooked by visions of wolves at the windows, and battling the prolific mouse invasions. Subsequent caretakers lasted no more than two years—until someone found Terry. Terry, one of those small men whose presence looms large, needed a place to retreat. Like Ron the squatter, he had found city life destructive. Battling addiction and suffering from a broken marriage, he took on the caretaking job as a healing retreat, meaning to stay for one year only. Terry's connection to Hemming Bay was his friend Fred—the two had roofed and framed houses, and they had driven cabs together in Red Deer, Alberta, during its oil boom. Fred had started an oyster farm just up the shore of Hemming Bay and had struck up good relationships with some of the community members.

When we first met Fred, he lived with his wife, Barb, and two dogs on his float home, which was attached to the floats on which the oysters grew, on ropes hung down at intervals. As I had experienced on my first dive into it, the water here was ice-cold. Not the best climate for oysters. But having an oyster lease allowed Fred to legally stay attached to the shore. The isolation and harsh winter conditions proved too much for Barb; she left a few years later. I remember seeing her boiling jars and canning salmon over a hot wood stove. (I was impressed—I sterilize my jars by running them through the dishwasher in the city.) Fred stayed on, making a modest income selling oysters, supplemented by working periodically at nearby fish farms and sometimes being employed in Hemming Bay building projects.

When his oysters started maturing—it takes five years from seeding for an oyster to reach consumable size—we were delighted to discover fishnet sacks of them left for us on Heartstone's little beach. Although Fred eventually abandoned oyster farming, we are still finding patches of them among the mud and rocks when the tide is low. Oysters can survive for as long as ten years.

## MUFFIN-TIN OYSTERS

For those who are not bold enough to simply eat them raw, with a squirt of lime juice and a gulp of vodka, here is Fred's recipe for baked oysters. Hint: to make them easier to shuck, first put them in a hot oven for five minutes.

Cut up bacon into 1– 2" pieces.
Put a piece of bacon on the bottom of each muffin-tin cup.

Plop a shucked oyster on top of each one, then top with another piece of bacon.

Bake for 20 minutes in a hot oven.

After removing them with a spoon, place on a paper towel–lined plate (to drain fat).

Drizzle with lemon.

Stick a toothpick through each oyster.

Serve with hot sauce, or ketchup mixed with horse-radish.

Return the oyster shells to the sea.

⚓

Fred and Terry remained friends throughout the twenty-five years that Terry served as Hemming Bay Community's caretaker. They fished, smoked and canned their catches together. A new community member hired them to build their cabin. They also built a hobbit house for Terry, made from Styrofoam blocks, covering its barrel-shaped roof with fishnet. Here, in his "bug-out," Terry could escape when the summer invasion of members with their friends and relatives took over the lodge.

When it was evident that Terry had lung cancer, his oldest son, Brenden, joined him. Terry took his last coughing breath in his upstairs nest at Hemming Bay Lodge, refusing to go to the hospital. Terry was not a drinker, at least not in the usual sense of that word. But we rarely saw him without a cup of coffee in one hand and a hand-rolled cigarette in the other. Marijuana was not legal during Terry's lifetime, and growing it on Hemming Bay property was not condoned by the community members, but Terry had a tin skiff and grew his illegal crop discreetly on the scattered islands of Hemming Lake. I wondered if some of the plants might have also thrived in Ron's abandoned garden.

The lodge caretaker's main job is to keep a supply of chopped wood in the two giant woodsheds. Luckily, abandoned logs from earlier logging operations were readily available. A wood-related memory I cherish from the time we spent in the community lodge with Vic's family and our combined six children was the "chain gang" arrangement of passing stove wood up one piece at a time from the big shed, up the stairs to the lodge back door, and into the wood-storage area under the kitchen counters. Vic would pass a chunk first to Lena, who passed it to Katie, who passed it to Amy, who passed it to Alex, who passed it to me, who passed it to Michael, who passed it to Tanya, who passed it to Woldy, who would stack it neatly in the kitchen wood bin. This work time was also fun time, with lots of mock groans, and sometimes songs with whose lyrics we took many liberties. "I've been working on the chain gang, all the live-long day!" "My lover was a logger, not just a common bum!" I loved quoting a favourite Tolstoy line to whoever would listen: "If every man chopped his own wood, we'd have no more war." The oldest girl child, Amy, added, "And every woman, too!"

Terry found his peace chopping wood, growing his own smokes, fishing, keeping the community's hydro system functioning (he seemed to be able to fix anything) and sometimes helping members build. Despite his suffering at the end, he got the peaceful death he wished for in his wilderness home.

A special connection I had with Terry was our annual jam exchange. Terry preserved jam made from huckleberries, which is quite labour-intensive: it is hard to fill a bucket with those bright red berries, which are only the size of BB pellets. What I brought to Terry in exchange was the marmalade I made every January—the only month of the year that Seville oranges can be found in Vancouver supermarkets. Making marmalade is also labour-intensive—taking three days to complete.

### ORANGE MARMALADE

2 pounds Seville oranges

1 large lemon

9 cups cold water

8 cups sugar

Slice the fruit as thin as possible, removing the seeds as you go.

Cover with water. Let sit for 24 hours.

Bring to a boil. Add sugar. Let sit for 24 hours.

Bring to a boil again. Simmer for about 2 hours.

Bring to a boil again, and boil hard for about ½ hour.

When the mixture is dark and thick, you can start pouring it into hot, clean jars.

Cover with melted paraffin wax.

(A friend from London says my dark marmalade looks and tastes like the marmalade sold at Harod's.)

I usually double this recipe, which produces 14 pickled-herring-size (250 gram) jars.

My marmalade was not only a favourite of Terry's, but was also considered a treat by Vic and Woldy. Before his departures for building stints, Woldy would pack at least two jars for the builders' breakfasts. As my home fills up with the scent of oranges for three days every January, I always remember the sweet-sour taste of Terry's huckleberry jam and wish I'd asked him for the recipe before he died.

My lengthier returns to Hemming Bay, a number of years after Alex's death, were largely initiated by a birth. Our daughter, Tanya, gave birth to a baby girl, our first grandchild, in 2001. Because Tanya was a single mom, Woldy and I helped out by having Ainsley every weekend and for most of the summer holidays. Our granddaughter brought new joy into our lives. I hushed her to sleep with the songs I had sung to our baby Alex, and as she grew, I read her his favourite children's stories—I hadn't given the books away. Like Alex, she learned the words to *Rumpelstiltskin, Snow White, The Bear Who Wanted to Stay a Bear,* and many others. When I reread *Higglety Pigglety Pop! or There Must Be More to Life*—in which Jennie the dog, who has her own bed, her own brush, her own pills and a master who loves her—runs away from home, looking for adventure, I remembered how Ainsley's mom left our home at the age of fourteen. Tanya, as I wrote previously, had said she wanted to find out what her birth mother loved more than her (heroin). She had many "adventures" on the street, and even time in juvenile detention, before becoming pregnant with Ainsley and deciding to settle down. A doctor, whom Woldy had employed for visits to his alternative school, threatened to take Tanya's baby if she were caught using. As far as I know, Tanya did abstain from drugs during her pregnancy. When baby Ainsley arrived, we purchased an apartment for the two of them. Tanya was able to pay part of the mortgage with occasional part-time jobs and income assistance. We loved spoiling her daughter, which Tanya seemed to resent. I made sure this child learned to swim.

Even though Ainsley was swimming by three years old, I was not in favour of bringing a toddler to the rough shores of Hemming Bay and a partially constructed Heartstone Lodge (no railing on the deck!). Anyway, she and I would just have been in the way of the workers. But by the time Ainsley was eight, Heartstone Lodge was habitable, so we invited a friend to come along for a holiday with her.

Ainsley's friend Michelle, a delicate Chinese girl, already a piano prodigy, had never left the city, never mind visiting the wilderness. I was surprised that her parents let us take her, and that they even dressed her appropriately. I was used to seeing Michelle in dainty dresses with matching stockings, but when we picked her up for our six-day Hemming Bay trip, she was in blue jeans, a pink-striped T-shirt and a matching baseball cap.

The girls turned tomboy even before we reached Hemming Bay, swinging from a suspended tire on the Rock Bay campground, our departure point from Vancouver Island, where we moored our twenty-five-foot transport boat. Woldy and I had sold the *Youngster*, our lovely motorsailer, finally agreeing that we could not be both sailors and part-time residents of Heartstone Lodge. Now our trip involved a ferry crossing to Nanaimo, a drive north of Campbell River to Rock Bay, and a twenty-minute crossing in the speedy transport vessel. This method of travel took a good part of the day, but not two days, as the trip had taken by motorsailer.

During their stay at Heartstone, Ainsley and Michelle fished, built a fort, picked berries and even scraped limpets off the rocks to make Hemming Bay escargot. All children seem to like garlic fried in butter, even with our snail-like limpets. (We didn't tell Michelle that limpets are also known as Chinese hats—and in any case, Michelle, who was born in Canada, may have never seen a Chinese hat.)

Despite the fabulous days, nights were a problem. There were no streetlights in Hemming Bay to soften the darkness, and at this point, there was no glass in the upstairs windows of Heartstone Lodge, where the girls were terrified by flying bats. There were tears! I moved my sleeping bag upstairs and slept on a foamy on the floor beside them.

Though we returned the delicate pianist in one piece, with only mosquito bites as scars, her parents declined to send her the following year. Instead, for the next few years, we managed to arrange our Ainsley time at Hemming Bay to coordinate with the visits of grandchildren belonging to another pair of aging community members, Bob and Sue Samson. The Samsons' daughter, Cynthia, who had been one of the children singing "Downdee, down, down!" with little Alex on our first Hemming Bay visit, now came with her husband, Alan, and their two children, Zoe and Jeremy. Although Cynthia and her family lived in San Francisco, the BC wilderness called them north every year. Zoe was the same age as our Ainsley, and her brother was just a year and a half younger.

The three children had no problem finding things to do. At the swimming rocks on Hemming Lake, they smeared each other with the beach's mud-like sand, climbed the rocks and then cannonballed off in running jumps. One afternoon they worked on a musical skit to perform in the evening for parents and grandparents. The fifteen hundred kilometres that separated their homes (Vancouver and San Francisco) did not mean that these preteens had different cultures. Thanks to TV, cellphones and computers, popular songs are shared throughout the world. The one they performed that night was commissioned by Metro Trains Melbourne to warn children about playing on railway tracks.

### "DUMB WAYS TO DIE"

Set fire to your hair.
Poke a stick at a grizzly bear.
Eat medicine that's out of date.
Use your private parts as piranha bait.

Dumb ways to die!
So many dumb ways to die!
Dumb ways to die-ie-ie!
So many dumb ways to die!

Get your toast out with a fork.
Do your own electrical work.
Teach yourself how to fly.
Eat a two-week-old unrefrigerated pie.

Dumb ways to die!
So many dumb ways to die!
Dumb ways to die-ie-ie!
So many dumb ways to die!

The lyrics go on for five more verses. I was amazed that all three children knew them by heart. They couldn't use their cellphones to check for missing lines—there was no reception at Hemming Bay!

Sitting on dilapidated patio chairs (anything that started to wear out at home was sent to Hemming Bay), an audience of two parents and four grandparents nearly rolled off the theatre's cliff setting as the kids mimed the "dumb ways to die."

Alex had died in a dumb way—falling through the seam of a plastic tennis court covering. Twenty years had now passed, and though his absence remained a constant source of sorrow, his means of death meant nothing to us. We could laugh with the children's assured sense of their own immortality. Laughing beside us were the parents and sister of Donald Samson, who, some would say, had also died in a dumb way. Bob and Sue's son had taken up base jumping, and he fell to his death from a bridge over the Royal Gorge near Colorado Springs when his parachute malfunctioned.

Yet we bereaved parents could laugh together. The spirited children and the wilderness setting relieved us for a time from our painful memories.

Last Christmas I bought a new resident for Hemming Bay—for Heartstone's fireplace mantel. It is a cast iron image of a raven in a First Nations style design. The raven is holding a red ball in its beak—illustrating the story of how Raven, the trickster, stole the sun. The card I attached to the Christmas wrapping was addressed to Woldy and Vic, the Heartstone builders.

After spending a month at our home in North Vancouver, Raven moved into Vic and Lee's home in Qualicum Beach on Vancouver Island. It was a time of crisis: Lee had just been diagnosed with bladder cancer. Opting not to undertake chemotherapy and the other conventional medical procedures, Lee instead followed her beliefs in the power of natural remedies, including shamanistic therapy. In a meditation experienced during her first session, brought on by the shaman's chanting, Lee had a vision of a raven, high up in a tree, watching over her. On her second visit to the shaman, the raven appeared again in her visioning, this time flying down to rest on her body at the cancerous spot. The bird then flew away with something in its beak.

At Lee's next ultrasound examination, the tumour was barely visible; it had shrunk from the size of a toonie to the size of a pea. Months later, an ultrasound showed only a calcium deposit.

In my work with bereaved parents, I have heard other tales of Raven as rescuer. As described in my poem "Raven Talks to Woldy," Woldy had a consoling experience of Alex talking to him, through Raven, from the Other Side. Our rational minds may scoff at tales of miraculous cures, but many of us still believe in Nature as the Great Healer.

When your heart feels heavy
as a stone and your eyes
have dried from too many tears,
turn heart and eyes seaward,
look for dolphins splashing
listen for kingfishers cackling
see how the sun reflects the waves
on cliffs,
turning stone itself
into shimmering laughter.

This poem came to me while I was sitting on the rock headland in front of Heartstone Lodge this past summer. Warmed by the sun, I fell into a meditative state, hypnotized by gently swaying dry grass somehow growing on stone, with moss as its soil. Across the bay, I could see Plum Tree Island, and I recalled young Tanya making a drawing of it with pencil crayons in a pointillist style. Hmm, where is that picture now? I must find it and hang it by my little desk in our Heartstone bedroom.

Would Tanya ever return to see it? I couldn't help but wonder. She had left us several years ago after marrying an Australian she had connected with through the Internet. In quick sequence, she had two babies by him while still living in the Vancouver area. Ainsley, who was used to being an only child, resented this intrusion and spent even more time with us. When the whole family—Tanya, her husband and the three children—moved to Australia, Ainsley was not happy. After a few months there, she asked to move back to live with us. And so she did—for six years—transforming Woldy and me from grandparents to full-time parents. She became a regular at Hemming Bay. Though she decided in her fourteenth year to move back to Australia to be with her mother, the beachfront fort she and her grandfather built still stands as a reminder of the good times she had there with us.

I regretted Ainsley's decision to leave our home but recognized her longing for her mother. Throughout her years with us, as hard as we tried to make her happy, she periodically wept in my arms, sobbing, "I miss my mother!" Her leaving left me feeling empty and depressed—*why can't I hang on to any of my children?* Again, I turned to writing as a means of self-therapy. My memoir, *Snapshots*, which describes my losses as a mother, ends on a happy note with tales of fun with a little granddaughter.

Heartstone Lodge, our refuge.

# A Mother Again

Over the years, Hemming Bay has come to represent a place of re-birth for both Woldy and me. Our hope in our later years was that it could also be a place of rebirth for our adopted son, Michael.

Michael's times on the streets of Vancouver, when he left our home at age fourteen, had spiralled into a life of crime and im-prisonment. Woldy and I visited him when he spent four years in a juvenile detention centre in the state of Washington. After his release at age twenty-one from a sentence of "juvie life," he returned briefly to our home in West Vancouver. When he ex-pressed discomfort at again living "at home," we subsidized a basement apartment for him in Vancouver. He held jobs briefly, but he soon returned to drugs and was arrested for car theft. Now that he was no longer a juvenile, his prison habitation was not comfortable. All three of us shed tears when we first visited him in a maximum-security facility. Our visit consisted of talking to an orange-clad Michael behind thick glass while guards looked on.

My relationship with Michael improved with distance. On one of Michael's periods of parole, he took a course in teaching ESL and then, with our financial help, flew to China to take a teaching post. There, in Chongqing, he excelled as a teacher, ris-ing to be the director of studies in the private language school where he was employed. He fell in love with a beautiful Chinese woman named Drew, and the young couple bonded with us on a two-week tour of China. Just a few months after that trip, Woldy and I returned to Chongqing to host Michael and Drew's wedding. Experiencing that festivity with Michael's teaching friends and Drew's relatives was one of the happiest times of my life.

One of the unhappiest times came two years later, when we received a call from Ottawa's foreign affairs office to tell us that Michael had been arrested in Chongqing for car theft. We were not entirely unprepared for this bad news. Drew had called a few times, telling us, between sobs, that Michael had left her and was now selling drugs on the streets of Chongqing. We knew he had been having trouble adjusting to his new role as husband and breadwinner in a foreign country, but we were unaware of what other pressures could have driven him back to his old life. I could only think that the power of his addiction again overcame him. His car thefts were not a means of getting rich, but a means of financing his habit.

What followed were eight years of imprisonment for Michael and eight years of anxiety for us. Our attempt to bring him back to Canada to serve his sentence here was to no avail. The Canadian government has no agreement with China regarding prisoner exchange. Drew visited him only once after his arrest. Though she had told us that we would always have a daughter in China, she had signed divorce papers and was no longer officially his wife. In a letter of apology to us, Michael wrote that losing her was harder even than the humility of imprisonment.

During his incarceration, Michael continued to teach ESL, an initiative he talked the prison authorities into. His students were fellow prisoners, some of them judges and lawyers. When we sought a Chinese lawyer after the news of Michael's arrest, we were told by a Chongqing student in Vancouver that criminal lawyers were rare in China. "If one of them argues with a police report, he will be arrested along with his client."

After Michael's trial and during his subsequent years of imprisonment, we were able to talk to him by phone once a week for ten minutes—*if* our call got through. And *if* the one English-speaking warden was available. Our calls were prefaced by a shouting voice: "No politics! No religion!" So, what were we to talk about? Michael could not tell us about his living conditions.

On our first call, Woldy asked, "How many are in your cell?"

"I can't talk about that," answered Michael, and an approving grunt was uttered by our listener.

We couldn't very well tell Michael about interesting plays we'd been attending, or dinner parties, or our recent trip to Mexico. The contrast between our lives and his was just too cruel. When we were in Mexico, or even at Hemming Bay (where there was now telephone reception in the community lodge), our calls would not be accepted—they had to come from our home number. During these silent times, Michael's plight weighed even more heavily on our minds and hearts.

After Woldy took the initiative to enroll Michael in an Open Learning program through Thompson Rivers University, we had substance for our conversations. Michael had obtained a general certificate for high school graduation during his time at the Maple Lane detention centre in Washington. Now he was studying first- and eventually second-year university courses with no help from a computer, a library or an instructor. To our amazement, Michael kept attaining A grades for his carefully handwritten essays and exams. I was delighted to discuss Faulkner, Austen and Nabokov with him, and I was delighted to read his well-crafted sentences, which came faxed to me from the prison, through the Canadian consulate in Chongqing, then to Ottawa's foreign affairs office. I would read them and then fax them to Thompson Rivers University. Some of the assignments got lost in this process, and Michael would patiently write them again.

When Michael took sociology or history courses, I turned the phone over to Woldy—I couldn't contribute in these fields.

After being released from the Chongqing prison at the age of thirty-nine, Michael was crippled from the many hours of sitting, perched on a two-foot-high stool and using his bed for a writing desk. His back pain from this unhealthy position was exacerbated when he was punished for pushing a fellow inmate. He had to sit on a stool in a tiny cell for a whole month. These confinements warped Michael's six-foot-four frame, so when he finally emerged and flew to Canada, he could only walk twenty steps at a time, and only with the help of a cane. Waiting for him at the airport, we expected to see him being pushed in the wheelchair we had ordered for his flight. Instead, I spotted a tall, thin man limping out of the arrivals exit. "Look, Woldy, I think that's Michael!" His bald head, which he had told us about in one of our phone calls, and his limping gait alerted me.

On our ride home, Michael was unable to sit erectly in our car but had to slump on his side. After sixteen hours of travel, he was in extreme pain. The next day, despite his discomfort, Michael accompanied Woldy to shop for some clothes. He had arrived in a gym-like outfit that an employee of the Canadian consulate in Chongqing had bought for him (with money we sent), and he was pulling a small suitcase on wheels. In the suitcase were all of Michael's possessions: the books that we had mailed to him for his university courses.

In the afternoon, Woldy took Michael to his sympathetic doctor. After a short examination, the GP said, "Go to Emergency and throw yourself on their mercy."

Most of us have either heard horror stories of waiting for hours at the emergency department, or we have experienced these waits ourselves. Well, Michael must have had a halo around his bald head when he limped into our local hospital just days after his arrival from China. Despite the absence of a BC Care Card, he was admitted to Emergency and given a CT scan. A young neurosurgeon on duty looked at it and said, "This pain can't go on. We'll operate tonight."

The doctor managed to find another compassionate professional, a young anesthesiologist, and they operated to remove Michael's herniated disc at eleven that night. At two in the morning, Dr. Mendelsohn phoned us to say the operation had been successful and that we should pick Michael up from the hospital at noon, as his private room cost three thousand dollars a day. He had to be in quarantine as a new arrival from China, and because of his long absence from this country, he had no medical coverage. What is amazing is that both the neurosurgeon and the anesthesiologist operated without expecting payment.

We had been waiting for Michael's release that summer, so we had made no travel plans. As soon as Michael walked out of the hospital on crutches, Woldy decided we should all go to Hemming Bay. I was not in favour. What could Michael do there? But then again, what could he do at home in our two-bedroom apartment? Either setting was so much better than where he had been for the past eight years that Michael said he would be happy wherever we took him.

On one of our phone calls to Michael near the end of his confinement in Yuzhou Prison, I asked what meal he was looking forward to after his arrival home. "Hemming Bay fish and chips," he said. I was surprised and pleased. We had not talked about Michael's childhood on any of our eight years of telephone chats, and I sometimes wondered if he had retained any of those early memories. Had years of drug use damaged his brain? It had been twenty-seven years since he had eaten Hemming Bay fish and chips—over a quarter of a century. I thought it could not be just the taste of beer batter and fresh cod that he remembered. That meal had been flavoured with the adventure of a fishing derby and the happy chatter of his siblings and cousins at the table. What a contrast to the water-soaked rice meals he had eaten in prison, his table peopled with some of the five thousand Chinese prisoners— Michael the only Westerner. We were able to pay for supplements of vegetables and dried meat, which he could get from the canteen. Otherwise, he might have died from malnutrition.

A week after Michael's back operation, we packed up for the trip to Hemming Bay. It was with some trepidation—Michael could not sit comfortably for long, and our road and ferry journey to Rock Bay, twenty-five miles north of Campbell River, where we moored our small speedboat to make the water journey across Johnstone Strait, would take hours. The last part of this trek was along a potholed gravel logging road (Rock Bay Road), and the crossing of Johnstone Strait was always rough, even in calm weather. Fortified by pain pills, Michael endured the five-hour journey, gritting his teeth and hanging on tightly to the car door armrest and then the sink counter in the bouncing boat. On arrival at the long docks that Woldy and Vic had built to access Heartstone, Michael was embarrassed that he could not help to carry the week's supply of food, clothing and bedding we unloaded from the boat. The surgeon had given him strict orders not to carry anything over twenty pounds for the next couple of months.

The memory of Michael's older brother, Alex, was embedded in Heartstone Lodge. Michael, of course, had not been part of its construction, and he expressed amazement when he first saw the sturdy structure hidden in the woods. We had adhered to the wilderness co-operative agreement stating that all dwellings must be at least fifty feet from the shoreline and that trees between a building and the shore must be left standing. So, approaching Heartstone by boat, one sees only forest. Now, coming up the forest path, I was seeing the miracle of Heartstone again through Michael's eyes.

Viewed from the trail, Heartstone seems to float on a sea of ferns. On either side and behind, the building is embraced by tall firs and cedars—its cedar-shake and board-and-batten exterior blend in, as if part of nature itself. Sitting on the deck that circles the house, weathered wooden chairs wait for visitors. Above them hangs a large copper gas lamp, once a decoration of an English pub, the Railway Tavern, now bearing the words Heartstone Lodge. Michael paused. I thought it was because of the difficulty of navigating an uphill rocky dirt path on crutches. But no, he was just looking, and repeating, "Wow! Wow! Wow!"

Vic had agreed to come with us for a few days to help open up Heartstone and haul our goods in. Once we had unpacked, rather than relaxing, the two brothers sussed out projects that still needed doing: the building of a generator shack and the installation of a hydroelectric system.

Michael, alone with me, observed that Woldy in this setting became the younger brother, acknowledging Vic's superior building knowledge—after all, Vic's business was construction. "I've never seen a situation where Dad was not in charge," Michael said, somehow amused. Then he added, "Well I guess if Alex was alive, I'd be the younger brother, too."

I busied myself with replenishing candle holders, turning my back so Michael wouldn't see my tears. Later, I thought, when we are not both feeling so vulnerable, and Michael's legs are stronger, I'll take him over to the creek mouth, where a tall fir holds a bronze plaque inscribed Alex's Landing. The co-operative members organized this memorial after Alex died, to commemorate where he pulled his kayak in after crossing Johnstone Strait alone. The landing is even named on charts of Hemming Bay.

What does someone recovering from a back operation do at Heartstone Lodge? Michael couldn't hike, swim, chop wood or even fish (to sit erect on a backless seat in a little dinghy was not an option). It turns out he could play Scrabble. In fact, as Woldy discovered in their first game together, Michael was an ace player. We had sent him a Scrabble set early on in his imprisonment. We wondered who he could play with? It turns out there was an incarcerated judge who wanted to improve his English. A brilliant man, he memorized the key Scrabble words (you know, those little two-letter ones you can use on a double or triple word square—*qi, ka*...). The judge and Michael played so often that they finally wore the letter imprints out.

"Why didn't you ask us to send another set?" I queried.

"Oh, the judge was transferred to another prison, and I didn't find anyone else to play with."

Both Woldy and I love playing Scrabble, so now Michael had two eager opponents. Though his parents won the occasional game, Michael won most often. He sometimes had three seven-letter words a game (each worth an extra fifty points), and while his dad and I were pleased if we scored over three hundred, Michael often scored over four hundred. *No, his brain has not been destroyed by drugs,* I mused. And I remembered the six-year-old boy we had adopted saying, "I'm no dummy!" when he couldn't keep up with his older brother's achievements.

⚓

Though we'd had a telephone relationship for eight years, which always ended with "I love you," it was strange to have this almost forty-year-old, six-foot-four body ever present and calling us Mom and Dad. When we parented Ainsley, we were Gramma and Grandpa. Now this was a kind of rebirth—reborn parents!

We said goodbye to Vic the day after our arrival at Heart-stone, making him promise to return for us in a week's time. That afternoon, Woldy took off in the skiff with his fishing equipment. A few hours later, he came up the trail carrying five beautiful rock-fish. Michael and I had peeled potatoes together in anticipation, and of course I remembered to open a beer to let it flatten for the batter. Woldy insisted that Michael watch him clean the fish, a lesson he hoped Michael would use in future summers. I made my little contribution of sauce, mixing together mayo and sweet green relish. After Woldy had smoked up the cabin with two pots of hot, crackling oil, popping one battered fillet after another into one, and scooping potato slices into the other, we lit candles, though it was not yet dark, and sat down to partake in this holy meal: cod fresh from the sea, coated in a batter of love.

Woldy (left) and Vic taking a break from the hard work of clearing and construction.

# EPILOGUE

It has now been two years since I wrote the last chapter of this book, which describes Woldy's and my trip to Hemming Bay with our son Michael, newly released from a Chinese prison. Our meal of fish and chips together in Heartstone Lodge made, I thought, a "happy ending"—and don't we all long for happy endings? Writing this epilogue now, I can assure readers that we were not filled with false hope. In the past two years, Michael has been employed on the weekends with the PHS Community Services Society in the Downtown East Side of Vancouver. There he cares for those who have been cast aside by society through their addictions or mental challenges—at times rescuing them from near-death overdoses. During the week, Michael serves as a youth worker for the Surrey school district on an anti-gang team. He relates well with the at-risk youth, having been there himself. After living with us for a year after his release, he now has his own apartment, car and cat. Once a week, he comes to our home to play Scrabble with his dad and stay for supper.

This summer, Michael will be coming with a friend to again holiday with us at Hemming Bay. Another visitor this year will be Jonny, Alex's best friend, who was with him when he died and, in his late teens, was the leader of the volunteer crew that laid the foundations for Heartstone Lodge. Jonny is now forty-four years old and will bring with him his wife and two small children. Later in the season, our grandchild, Ainsley, will come for a few days with a friend of hers. At age nineteen, she has decided that life in Canada suits her more than life in Australia. So Heartstone will be well used and appreciated.

Vic and Woldy continue to work when they arrive, dropping trees that have rotted and that endanger the structure, installing solar panels for power, and repairing the three hundred feet of dock (which they bring in each fall under the high tide of a full moon to protect it from winter storms, returning in spring to move it out again). Now that the brothers are in their seventies, I wonder how long this kind of activity can be sustained? Though Vic's three daughters have married, they live scattered across the globe. Recently, Vic helped me with this question about the future of Heartstone with an old Chinese saying: "Until a man finishes building his house, he is not ready to die." Meanwhile, this woman is happy washing windows.

# Acknowledgements

Thanks to the founding and continuing members of the Hemming Bay Community for their foresight and energy in maintaining this piece of wilderness on East Thurlow Island.

Thanks to the building brothers, Woldy and Vic, and all their helpers who have hand-crafted Heartstone Lodge to be the unique and welcoming home-in-the-woods it is.

Thanks to my children and grandchild for teaching me how to be a mother.

Thanks to Donaleen Saul and Gordon Thomas for their sensitive readings of this manuscript in the rough.

Thanks to the editors at Caitlin Press for pushing me to tell more of my story.

Thanks to my husband, Woldy, for his patience and sustaining love.

# About the Author

Photo Woldy Sosnowsky

After teaching poetry as a college instructor for many years, Cathy Sosnowsky turned to writing for solace after the loss of her three children, one to a fatal and tragic accident and two to addiction. Her poetry collection, *Holding On: Poems for Alex* (*Creative Connections Publishing,* 2001), traces her passage through grief and her memoir, *Snapshots: A Story of Love, Loss and Life* (Granville Island Publishing, 2010), includes the story of losing her two adopted children to drugs. Cathy's writing has also appeared in the *Vancouver Sun*, the *Globe and Mail*, the *Georgia Straight*, and *Pacific Yachting*. She has presented about grief and writing worldwide, conducts writing workshops, and is the chapter leader and newsletter editor of the North Shore Compassionate Friends, a parents' bereavement group. *Finding Heartstone* is a testimony to the healing power of writing, home cooking, and nature. Cathy lives in North Vancouver, BC, with her husband, Woldy.

Woldy carves a prize and Alex makes a sign for a fishing derby.